GLACIER DAY HIKES

by Alan Leftridge

FARCOUNTRY
PRESS

Acknowledgments

There are several people who deserve special recognition for helping me complete this book. I am grateful for my daughter and hiking partner, Miranda, for the many hours she spent on the trail and for the ways she shared her excitement of discovery. I want to recognize my son, Dustin, for his encouragement. I am thankful for my eldest daughter, Nicole, for her inspiration. I also want to thank my mother, Lorraine Leftridge, for her support. Dr. Linda Duvanich reviewed the text and provided insightful recommendations. Dave Dahlen, Chief of Interpretation, Glacier National Park, provided valuable assistance. I wish to thank several people at Farcountry Press for giving me the opportunity to write this guide: Kathy Springmeyer for suggesting this project; Bob Smith for drawing the maps you see herein; and Charlene Patterson for her thorough final edit of the book. Finally, I wish to thank the many Glacier National Park interpreters, rangers, concessionaires, and Glacier Natural History Association employees who provided information about the trails.

About the Author

Alan Leftridge has been a seasonal naturalist in Yellowstone National Park and a wilderness ranger in the Mission Mountains Wilderness of Montana. He earned a Bachelor of Science degree in biology at Central Missouri State University, a Ph.D. in science education at Kansas State University, and a teaching credential from the University of Montana. During the last 25 years he taught high school science in West Yellowstone, science courses at Miami University, Ohio, and environmental education classes at Humboldt State University, California. He is currently the executive editor of *The Interpreter*, the magazine of the National Association for Interpretation. Alan lives south of Glacier National Park in the Swan Valley.

Through the National Association for Interpretation he has earned the distinction of being named a Certified Interpretive Guide trainer. He conducts guide training and interpretive writing workshops throughout the United States.

Front cover photograph © John Reddy
Back cover and color section photography © Alan Leftridge

ISBN 10: 1-56037-248-6
ISBN 13: 978-1-56037-248-6

Text © 2003 Alan Leftridge
© 2003 Farcountry Press
This book may not be reproduced in whole or in part by any means (with the exception of short quotes for the purpose of review) without the permission of the publisher. For more information on our books write Farcountry Press, P.O. Box 5630, Helena, MT 59604; call (800) 821-3874; or visit www.farcountrypress.com.
Printed in Canada. Created, designed, and published in the USA.

10 09 08 07 06   2 3 4 5 6

Table of Contents

North Fork Hikes

Introduction

Glacier National Park is too big and too beautiful to take in during one visit. It is too far-flung and diverse to view in a day or two. The entire park is worth seeing, and the best way to see Glacier National Park is to get out of your car and experience its sights, sounds, and fragrances up close and personally. This can be done via a hike.

"Glaciered" National Park might be a better descriptive name for this international treasure. The park was named not for the small glaciers in the park today, but for the massive ancient glaciers that carved the landscape. The glaciers you see today are not remnants of the ancient glaciers, but formed later. Since the time of the great glacial episode 18,000 years ago, countless smaller glaciers have formed and disappeared in a somewhat cyclical process. The glaciers you see today are one-half or one-third their size of a century ago.

Glacier National Park has an annual visitation of 1.6 million people. On any given day at the height of the visitor season in July or August 2,500 to 3,500 people may visit Logan Pass. About 98 percent of the visitors see the park from Going-to-the-Sun Road or other roads within the park. Very few visitors venture as far as 1 mile off the roads on the trails. Early park naturalist George C. Ruhle, who named the highway "Going-to-the-Sun," stated, "At first this was primarily a walking and horseback-riding park. . . . Now they skim through it in an automobile and they cling to it like a shipwrecked sailor to a raft."

Glacier National Park has approximately 750 miles of maintained trails. Even in the height of the tourist season there are many trails in the park on which you will encounter few, if any, fellow travelers. This guide attempts to describe some of these less-used trails and at the same time include the "must do" premier hikes. Some hikes are considered "premier" because of the outstanding features you can access in a short distance and with little effort.

What is a day hike? For the purposes of this guide a day hike ranges from 1 mile to 16 miles round trip. Why would someone want to day hike? It is obvious that many people hike for exercise, while others want to reach particular destinations in the park. There are a few other people who are not interested in reaching a destination but want to experience the wonders along the trail. These visitors intend to photograph, identify mushrooms, mosses, butterflies, wildflowers, or animal tracks, or add to their life list of birds. Some find it enjoyable to people-watch.

Explore and enjoy. Leave nature as you found it. Keep a record of your activities for your next visit.

And return often to experience the beauty and solitude only Glacier can offer.

How to Use This Book

Much effort has been made to accurately depict the character of the trails described herein. By their very nature outdoor activities carry a degree of risk. Sound judgment on your behalf will minimize potential hazards. Assume responsibility for your own actions and safety. Check with park personnel to verify the condition of the trail you intend to take.

There are more than 750 miles of maintained trails in Glacier National Park. There were several criteria used in selecting the trails included in this book: varying ecosystems in the park, distance relative to providing optimum experience, trail conditions, and recognition that most readers of this book are novice hikers; finally there are several trails that would be considered "must do" if you want to truly experience Glacier.

Level of Difficulty: The trails are rated as easy, moderate, or strenuous. The descriptions are based on terrain and trail conditions, not the length of the trail. Easy walks will have little elevation gain and will be on well-maintained, soft-surfaced trails. Strenuous hikes will have terrain diversity and often include walking over broken, loose rock surfaces. An easy trail may be lengthy and accomplished by anyone, with ample time. A strenuous trail may be short but demanding. All of the trail destinations in this guide are considered day hikes.

Distance: All distances are represented in round trip miles from the trailhead and back. Distances were established using published sources from the National Park Service.

Duration: Travel times are approximations. I hiked all of the trails in this guide averaging 2 miles an hour. Two miles is the distance an average adult would expect to cover in an hour, even with frequent stops to discover and experience the wonders of the surroundings.

Best time of year: Most of the trails in Glacier National Park are either snow-covered or wet until mid-June. Access to the these trails is difficult or impossible by late-October. This section indicates when, on average, you can expect to access the trails. For many of the trails, however, the most comfortable time of year is when the trail is dry and biting insect populations are low. This often means waiting until mid-August.

Hiking directions: There are more than 750 miles of established trails in the park. There are also numerous unmarked, unmaintained, or abandoned trails. Some trails crisscross one another. The Park Service is updating signage at trail junctions to include metric measurements. This process is not complete, and the current information available along some trails can be confusing. Also, some trails are designated with more than one name. The hiking directions and notes in this book are intended to clarify potentially confusing situations.

Special attention: Please heed these considerations. They are based on my experience on the trails.

Notes: The notes include a description of the trail as well as information regarding the natural and cultural history of the area. The notes are intended to be an invitation to explore. Experience the wonders of Glacier National Park on your own terms. However, please stay on the trail. Build memories, and plan to return often.

Trail Map Legend

Primary paved road	Ranger station
Secondary paved road	Ranger station (infrequently staffed)
Gravel or dirt road	Trailhead
Featured hiking trail	Self-guiding trail
Other hiking trails	Boat tours/rentals
Distance indicator (2.5mi 4.0km)	Campground
Contour lines (7200)	Primitive campground
Trailhead parking	Backcountry campground
Building (Visitor Center)	Picnic area
Bridge	Horseback riding (rental, guided tour)
Continental Divide	Food service
Waterfall	Lodging
Marsh	Boat launch
Glacier/snowfield	Wheelchair accessible trail
Mine site (Cracker Mine)	Lookout tower

Contour lines showing elevation gain on individual trail maps are to help you assess trail difficulty. Each contour line connects all points at the same elevation; numbers on the heavier lines state exact elevations in feet. The elevation interval between contour lines appears on each map—note that our maps use different intervals, depending on the trail. The closer together contour lines are, the steeper the trail's ascent or descent.

Refer to United States Geological Survey (USGS) maps for more detailed representations. They are sold in some outdoors stores; via mail from USGS Earth Science Informations Services, Box 25286, Denver, CO 80225 (phone 888-ASK-USGS); or see the USGS website at http://mcmcweb.er.usgs.gov/topomaps/ordering_maps.html

Trail Locator Map

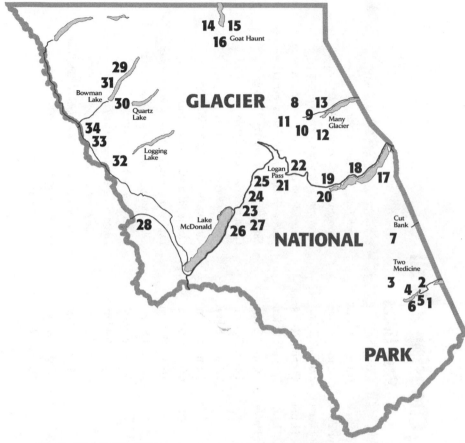

Two Medicine/Cut Bank Hikes
1. Scenic Point
2. Running Eagle Falls
3. Oldman Lake
4. Upper Two Medicine Lake
5. Appistoki Falls
6. Aster Park
7. Medicine Grizzly Lake

Swiftcurrent/Goat Haunt Hikes
8. Iceberg Lake
9. Swiftcurrent Lake loop
10. Grinnell Valley
11. Swiftcurrent Valley
12. Cracker Lake
13. Appekunny Falls
14. Rainbow Falls
15. Goat Haunt Overlook
16. Kootenai Lakes

Going-to-the-Sun Hikes
17. Red Eagle Lake
18. Otokomi Lake
19. Baring Falls
20. St. Mary Falls and Virginia Falls
21. Hidden Lake
22. Garden Wall
23. Johns Lake Loop
24. Trail of the Cedars
25. Avalanche Lake
26. Fish Lake
27. Snyder Lake

North Fork Hikes
28. Forest and Fire Nature Trail
29. Bowman Lake
30. Quartz Lake loop
31. Numa Ridge Lookout
32. Logging Lake
33. Hidden Meadow
34. Covey Meadow Loop

Choosing a Trail
Easy Hikes

Trail Number and Name	Area	Round Trip Distance	Highlights	Page No.
2. Running Eagle Falls	Two Medicine/Cut Bank	0.3 mi/0.5 km	"Trick Falls," two falls in one	17
5. Appistoki Falls	Two Medicine/Cut Bank	1.2 mi/1.9 km	Furious waterfall cutting a slender canyon	26
9. Swiftcurrent Lake Loop	Swiftcurrent/Goat Haunt	2.6 mi/4.2 km	Panoramic lake views from all angles	37
10. Grinnell Valley	Swiftcurrent/Goat Haunt	13.0 mi/20.8 km	Waterfalls, wildlife, flowers, and a glacier, too	39
11. Swiftcurrent Valley	Swiftcurrent/Goat Haunt	7.0 mi/11.2 km	Redrock Falls, a chain of lakes, expansive valley	43
14. Rainbow Falls	Swiftcurrent/Goat Haunt	2.0 mi/3.2 km	Elongated cascade with crystal pools	54
19. Baring Falls	Going-to-the-Sun	1.4 mi/2.3 km	Great photo op. with dippers	69
20. St. Mary Falls	Going-to-the-Sun	2.4 mi/3.8 km	Multi-sensory experience	71
20. Virginia Falls	Going-to-the-Sun	3.6 mi/5.8 km	Canyon itself is worth the hike	71
21. Hidden Lake	Going-to-the-Sun	6.0 mi/9.6 km	"Top of the world" alpine scenery	74
22. The Garden Wall	Going-to-the-Sun	7.0 mi/11.2 km	Explosion of wildflower colors, lots of water	78
23. Johns Lake Loop	Going-to-the-Sun	3.0 mi/4.8 km	Old growth, Johns Lake, McDonald Creek	82
24. Trail of the Cedars	Going-to-the-Sun	0.7 mi/1.1 km	Silence and memorable views	86
25. Avalanche Lake	Going-to-the-Sun	4.0 mi/6.4 km	Large glacier-fed lake, beautiful forests	90
26. Fish Lake	Going-to-the-Sun	6.0 mi/9.6 km	Deep forest fairyland setting	94
28. Forest and Fire Nature Trail	North Fork	0.9 mi/1.4 km	Was the Huckleberry Mountain Nature Trail	102
33. Hidden Meadow	North Fork	2.4 mi/3.8 km	Isolated meadow, lots of wildlife	117
34. Covey Meadow Loop	North Fork	2.0 mi/3.2 km	Young forest environment	120

Moderate Hikes

Trail Number and Name	Area	Round Trip Distance	Highlights	Page No.
1. Scenic Point	Two Medicine/Cut Bank	7.0 mi/11.2 km	Stunning 360-degree view	14
3. Oldman Lake	Two Medicine/Cut Bank	13.0 mi/20.8 km	Arresting alpine beauty	18
4. Upper Two Medicine Lake	Two Medicine/Cut Bank	10.0 mi/16.0 km	Twin Falls, inspiring views of glaciated valley	22
6. Aster Park	Two Medicine/Cut Bank	3.8 mi/6.0 km	Paradise Point, Aster Falls	29
8. Iceberg Lake	Swiftcurrent/Goat Haunt	9.5 mi/15.2 km	Glaciated peaks and cold isolated lake	34
13. Appekunny Falls	Swiftcurrent/Goat Haunt	2.0 mi/3.2 km	Tall, narrow waterfall	51
15. Goat Haunt Overlook	Swiftcurrent/Goat Haunt	2.0 mi/ 3.2 km	Alpine flowers, inspirational view	56
16. Kootenai Lakes	Swiftcurrent/Goat Haunt	5.0 mi/8.0 km	Deep forest, Waterton River, moose	59
27. Snyder Lake	Going-to-the-Sun	8.8 mi/14.0 km	Small lake in a sheltered valley	97
29. Bowman Lake	North Fork	14.0 mi/22.4 km	Many miles of shoreline to discover	104
32. Logging Lake	North Fork	8.8 mi/14.0 km	Recently fire-altered forest, remote lake	114

Strenuous Hikes

Trail Number and Name	Area	Round Trip Distance	Highlights	Page No.
7. Medicine Grizzly Lake	Two Medicine/Cut Bank	13.0 mi/20.8 km	Cut Bank Creek, Atlantic Falls	34
12. Cracker Lake	Swiftcurrent/Goat Haunt	13.0 mi/20.8 km	Mining remnants, waterfalls, colorful lake	46
17. Red Eagle Lake	Going-to-the-Sun	15.0 mi/24.0 km	Suspension bridges, flower meadows	62
18. Otokomi Lake	Going-to-the-Sun	11.0 mi/17.6 km	Extraordinary colored rocks	66
30. Quartz Lake Loop	North Fork	12.8 mi/20.5 km	Chain of lakes	107
31. Numa Ridge Lookout	North Fork	10.6 mi/16.9 km	Fantastic panoramic views	110

Trail Tips

These considerations will enhance your hiking experiences in Glacier.

◆ Be thoughtful of others.

◆ Plan ahead and prepare. Visit a ranger station or a visitor center to inquire about recent animal sightings and trail conditions. Check the trailhead for ranger-posted alerts.

◆ Many trails are lined with dense undergrowth. The plant leaves retain moisture after a rain or from morning dew. Non-water-repellent closing absorbs the water as you brush against the undergrowth. Wear water-repellent clothing if hiking in the early morning or after rainfall.

◆ Bring a camera and/or journal to record your experiences.

Remember

◆ Walk single file in order to lessen the erosion caused by trail widening.

◆ Travel on established, durable, designated trails. Shortcuts can be dangerous and may increase erosion.

◆ Leave no trace. Leave what you find, unless it is something that someone else has carelessly misplaced. Pack out any food containers or food wrappers that you take with you.

◆ Yield to uphill hikers if the trail is a single pathway.

◆ Yield to stock users. Stand on the downhill side and away from the trail.

◆ Dogs are not permitted in the backcountry.

◆ Bicycles are allowed only on designated trails.

◆ Respect the needs of wildlife. Allow wildlife to step off the trail before continuing your hike.

Hiking in Bear Country

The best way to avoid a confrontation with a bear is to take a few precautions:

◆ Hike during the midmorning to midafternoon. These are the hours that bears are least active.

◆ Hike with companions.

◆ Make your presence known, particularly near blind turns in the trail and if you are walking into the wind. Whistle, sing, and clap your hands.

- Inquire at ranger stations if bears have been frequenting the area you wish to explore.
- Stay at least 100 feet from a bear.
- Never approach a bear.
- Move with slow, deliberate motions if you encounter a bear.
- If a grizzly is on the trail, consider completing your hike another day.

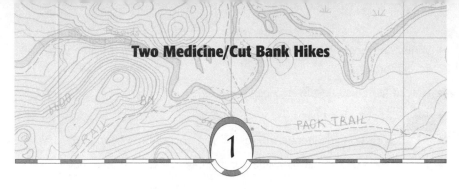

Scenic Point

This trail takes you to a windswept bald summit that provides an exceptional 360-degree view of southeastern Glacier National Park, the plains to the east, and the Great Bear Wilderness to the south. The hike to 7,522-foot Scenic Point is possibly the most sought-after in the Two Medicine Valley.

Level of difficulty: Moderate.

Distance: 7 miles round trip.

Duration: 4–5 hours.

Best time of year: July–October.

Trailhead: The Scenic Point Trailhead is 0.25 mile east of the Two Medicine Campground on Two Medicine Road.

Hiking directions: The sign at the trailhead designates this as the "Mount Henry Trail." The trail begins narrow, relatively flat, and winding. At 0.6 mile you come to the Appistoki Falls Trail. The Appistoki Falls overlook is 200 feet up this spur trail. Special care should be taken at the overlook since there is no guardrail that might save you from a devastating tumble. Soon after the Appistoki Falls spur trail junction the trail to Scenic Point begins to climb and switchback up the east side of the Appistoki Creek drainage. At the 2 mile mark you pass through a subalpine fir forest and break out onto a ridge above timberline. The trail climbs through a saddle and wraps around the north mountainside to the east. Soon you will see a signpost in the treeless distance. This sign gives you final directions to Scenic Point.

Special attention: You should begin this hike in the early morning hours during the warm summer months. The sun can be unsympathetic on the exposed southwest-facing trail. The wind can be intense at Scenic Point. Expect to find the conditions severe at the Point if the weather is blustery on the valley floor.

Notes: You immediately enter an established subalpine fir/spruce/pine forest. The understory includes beargrass (a lily) and several grass species. Watch for ruffed grouse and listen for nuthatches, chickadees, and Clark's nutcrackers.

The trail climbs on rocky limestone fragments through subalpine and alpine environments. The trail passes through small pockets of subalpine firs, western white pines, and limber pines and then breaks out onto rocky windswept slopes.

At 2 miles you will pass over a saddle and see Scenic Point in the distance to the east. From the saddle to Scenic Point you will be traversing a fellfield. This describes an alpine tundra environment with 30 to 50 percent rock surface. It is also characterized by low-growing pin-cushion-shaped and flat perennial plants. Wildflowers such as carpet pink, snow cinquefoil, forget-me-nots, and purple saxifrage thrive in this windswept, arid environment, growing in thin, nutrient-deficient topsoil. Some of these plants can live to be hundreds of years old. The last 100 yards of your ascent to Scenic Point is not on a trail but over the fellfield. Take special care not to step on the wildflowers. Look for ripple marks and mud cracks in the red argillite rocks at the top of Scenic Point. Also notice the different-colored lichens growing on the rocks.

Gaze east from Scenic Point across the vast prairie of Montana. The mountains in the far distance in front of you are the Sweetgrass Hills. Between the Hills and your position is the town of Browning. Below you and to your right is East Glacier. Farther south is the Great Bear Wilderness, part of the Bob Marshall Wilderness complex. The mountains closest to you to the south are Bison Mountain, Mount Henry at 8,847 feet, and Appistoki Peak at 8,164 feet. Behind you is Sinopah Mountain at 8,271 feet and the jagged peaks of Mount Helen and Flinsch Peak framing the conspicuous Dawson Pass. Rising Wolf Mountain, 9,513 feet in elevation, dominates your view across the valley to the northwest.

Lichens

At this altitude it is the lichens that are most accountable for relentlessly breaking down rocks into soil. Here, above timberline, lichens dominate the plant community. They are able to grow on bare rock, even at this altitude. The lichens produce acids that gradually make crevices in the rock surface. Small quantities of the decaying lichens and bits of dust collect in these crevices. From this action simple soil is formed. After rain, this soil will hold small quantities of water. This produces the conditions that encourage mosses to grow. The plant community succession moves on through the eons until summits like Scenic Point are reduced to low hills.

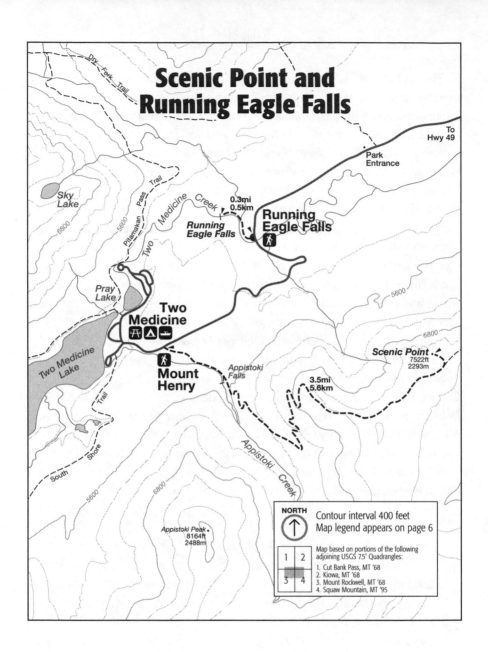

Scenic Point and Running Eagle Falls

Dry Fork Trail

Sky Lake

6800

Pitamakan Pass Trail

Two Medicine Creek

5600

0.3mi 0.5km

Running Eagle Falls

Running Eagle Falls

To Hwy 49

Park Entrance

5600

Pray Lake

Two Medicine

Mount Henry

Appistoki Falls

Two Medicine Lake

South Shore Trail

5600

6800

Appistoki Creek

Scenic Point
7522ft
2293m

6800

3.5mi 5.6km

Appistoki Peak
8164ft
2488m

NORTH
↑

Contour interval 400 feet
Map legend appears on page 6

1	2
3	4

Map based on portions of the following adjoining USGS 7.5' Quadrangles:

1. Cut Bank Pass, MT '68
2. Kiowa, MT '68
3. Mount Rockwell, MT '68
4. Squaw Mountain, MT '95

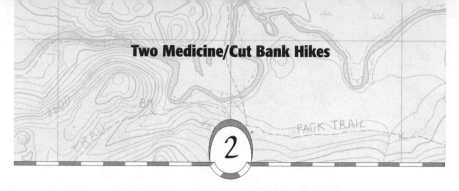

Running Eagle Falls

Running Eagle Falls is a "must see" feature in Glacier National Park. It is worthy of a visit during each of your trips to the Two Medicine area.

Level of difficulty: Easy.

Distance: 0.3 mile round trip.

Duration: 1 hour.

Best time of year: July–September.

Trailhead: The Running Eagle Falls Trailhead is 1 mile west of the Two Medicine entrance station. There is ample parking for several cars.

Hiking directions: There are two possible pathways to follow. One near the bridge is wide, gentle, and not paved. The other pathway begins near the center of the parking lot and is paved. The trails converge before arriving at the confluence of Dry Creek and Two Medicine Creek.

Special attention: The Glacier Natural History Association and the National Park Service have provided a Running Eagle Falls Nature Trail guide. You can acquire the guide for 50 cents at the trailhead.

Notes: The short walk to Running Eagle Falls is a refreshing stroll through a lush riparian forest environment. The trail guide will tell you the story of Running Eagle, in English and in the Blackfeet language. The guide also provides background information on the Blackfeet People's traditional and medicinal uses for some of the plants you will encounter along the trail. The guide will enhance your appreciation of this naturally beautiful and culturally rich area.

Running Eagle Falls is close to the trailhead, making it accessible to almost any hiker. Because of its geology, this unique waterfall changes depending on the water volume in the creek.

Early morning offers the best opportunity to photograph this unique waterfall. You will be photographing into the sun by midafternoon.

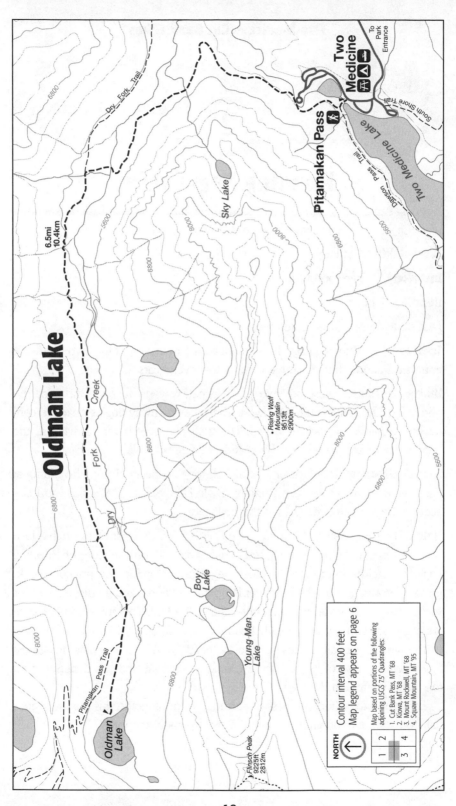

Oldman Lake

Two Medicine

To Park Entrance

Pitamakan Pass

Two Medicine Lake

South Shore Trail

Dawson Pass Trail

Dry Fork Trail

Sky Lake

6.5mi
10.4km

Fork Creek

Dry

Rising Wolf Mountain
9513ft
2900m

Boy Lake

Young Man Lake

Pitamakan Pass Trail

Flinsch Peak
9225ft
2812m

Oldman Lake

NORTH

Contour interval 400 feet
Map legend appears on page 6

Map based on portions of the following adjoining USGS 7.5' Quadrangles:

1. Cut Bank Pass, MT '68
2. Kiowa, MT '68
3. Mount Rockwell, MT '68
4. Squaw Mountain, MT '95

| 1 | 2 |
| 3 | 4 |

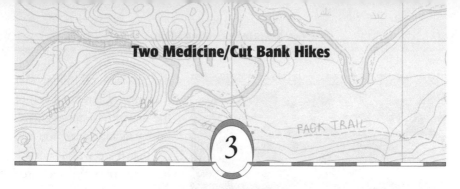

Oldman Lake

Whether shimmering in the sunlight or reflecting the images of the surrounding mountains, Oldman Lake strikes a vivid contrast with the sheer cliffs that enclose it on three sides.

Level of difficulty: Moderate.

Distance: 13 miles round trip.

Duration: 6–7 hours.

Best time of year: July–October.

Trailhead: There are two access points to Oldman Lake from the Two Medicine Valley. One is next to the entrance station on Two Medicine Road. The other is at Two Medicine Campground. This guidebook addresses the walk beginning at the campground. The trailhead is at the end of Loop A at Two Medicine Campground. The trail is marked with a sign that reads "Oldman Lake and North Shore Trail." Cross over a footbridge and enter the forest on the other side of Pray Lake.

Hiking directions: The trail splits after crossing the footbridge at the outlet of Pray Lake. Take the right fork on the Pitamakan Pass Trail.

Special attention: The trail to Oldman Lake skirts the exposed base of Red Mountain. You will need to carry extra water on a hot summer day.

Notes: You enter a multi-aged, mature, spruce-fir forest with luxuriant undergrowth. This riparian area is full of forest-dwelling birds such as nuthatches, chickadees, robins, flickers, and gray jays. The flora is characteristically Montana, including mountain asters, beargrass, buffaloberry, snowberry, saskatoon, wild rose, harebell, and paintbrush.

At first the trail swings to the north and wraps around the base of Rising Wolf Mountain. The remainder of your walk to Oldman Lake will take you halfway around this colossal 9,513-foot mass.

The trail immediately begins a slow ascent toward your destination. As you wind your way around the mountain you will encounter more aspen, Douglas fir, and subalpine fir trees. A new avalanche chute that crosses the trail on the

An unnamed waterfall along Dry Creek.

eastern face of Rising Wolf Mountain will remind you of the awesome forces generated by sliding snow. You can tell that there was a substantial snowpack in the area when the slides occurred because few trees are uprooted; most of the damage happened to the upper portions of the trees. You will then step back into forest that has not experienced a dramatic snow episode. This area has a healthy population of red squirrels. You will hear them chattering and dropping Douglas fir and subalpine fir cones to the forest floor.

The trail works its way to the bottomland of the Dry Fork of Two Medicine Creek, commonly called Dry Creek. This riparian habitat hosts a number of songbird species including white-crowned sparrows, warbling vireos, and orange-crowned warblers. Listen for their songs and calls during the morning and afternoon hours.

At 2 miles the trail crosses Dry Creek. Depending on the time of year the creek could be dry or full. After crossing Dry Creek you come to a trail junction announcing the directions to Dry Fork Trail, Oldman Lake, Pitamakan Pass, and Two Medicine Campground. You are 4 miles from Oldman Lake.

The trail now continues directly up the valley toward Oldman Lake. The trail moves into and out of a lodgepole pine forest that has a healthy understory of low-growing huckleberry bushes. The understory displays dramatic orange and crimson in late summer.

Near the 3 mile mark you cross a creek on a footbridge that drains an unnamed lake at the base of 9,377-foot Red Mountain. You then climb up a hill through dense forest before you break out into a clearing that affords a view of a picturesque waterfall on Dry Creek. This unnamed waterfall would be best photographed in the early afternoon.

For the next 3 miles you will be walking through the effects of the Dry Fork Forest Fire of 1925. The fire left large open areas that have not yet recovered. Only small stands of subalpine fir have become established on this south-facing mountainside.

At the 5 mile mark you approach a draw that is made up almost exclusively of red argillite. This area has a seasonal cascading waterfall. The effect is dramatic whether water is flowing over the mudstone or if the creek is dry.

At 6 miles you come to a sign that indicates Oldman Lake is to the left and Pitamakan Pass to the right. Head toward Oldman Lake. The last mile is though a forest that is dominated by whitebark pine that has been almost completely killed by the whitebark pine blister rust disease from Europe. The open canopy has provided ideal conditions for huckleberry growth.

Oldman Lake is a moderately sized cirque lake sitting at the eastern base of 8,781-foot Mount Morgan. To your right is Pitamakan Pass and 9,225-foot Flinsch Peak.

Looking to the east as you leave Oldman Lake, you will see the typical U-shaped topography of a glaciated valley. Also, high on the flanks of Red Mountain and Rising Wolf Mountain you can see the effects of the work of glaciers as they carved out the cirques and bowls near the tops of the peaks.

The Red Squirrel

The red squirrel is a denizen of the forests of Glacier National Park. Locally known as the pine squirrel, these tree acrobats delight visitors with their endearing antics. You may detect pine squirrels by sight or sound. Their noisy chattering is a territorial cry. With a home range of less than 200 yards and populations of two squirrels to 3 acres, their territories easily overlap. They are constantly reminding their neighbors to stay clear. As you walk down the trail you might notice mushroom caps broken off. Mushrooms make up part of the diet of the red squirrel. You may also notice a squirrel carry a mushroom cap up a pine tree, where the squirrel may take a couple of bites and lodge the mushroom in a tree branch, caching it for a future meal. A loud chattering cry will warn the squirrel's neighbors to stay away from the mushroom, before he leaps away to find more food.

Red squirrels do not hibernate. They will make burrows through Glacier's deep snowpack searching for food they cached. They can live up to ten years if they elude their common predators: owls, martens, foxes, and bobcats.

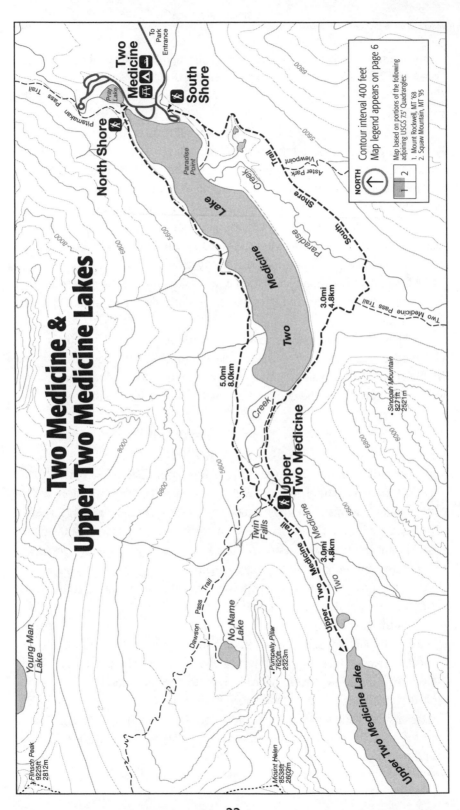

Two Medicine &
Upper Two Medicine Lakes

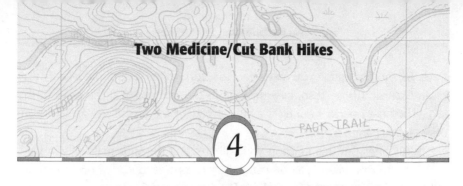

Upper Two Medicine Lake

The walk to Upper Two Medicine Lake will give you the opportunity to survey the natural and cultural history of the Two Medicine Valley. You will gain a different perspective of this beautiful valley and get the feeling that you are deep in the Glacier wilderness.

Level of difficulty: Moderate.

Distance: 10 miles round trip.

Duration: 5–6 hours.

Best time of year: June–October.

Trailhead: The trailhead is at the end of Loop A at Two Medicine Campground. The trail is marked as "Oldman Lake and North Shore Trail."

Hiking directions: Follow the North Shore Trail. The trail is well maintained, easy to follow, and parallels the north shore of Two Medicine Lake.

Notes: The first 0.25 mile of the trail will provide you with good views of the lake and Two Medicine Camp Store as well as vistas of the immense 9,513-foot Rising Wolf Mountain to the north. Across the lake and in front of you is the much photographed Sinopah Mountain at 8,271 feet. The mountains to the south include Painted Tepee Peak, 7,650 feet, Never Laughs Mountain at 7,641 feet, and Appistoki Peak at 8,164 feet.

As you venture along the trail you will alternate between crossing avalanche chutes and walking through a coniferous forest of lodgepole pine, Douglas fir, and subalpine fir trees. Deciduous trees that dominate the mountainside include willows, mountain maples, black cottonwoods, alders, and aspens. The profuse understory features serviceberry, mountain aster, thimbleberry, paintbrush, harebell, lupine, beargrass, snowberry, sumac, and fireweed.

At 3.3 miles you will come to a junction with a trail to the right ascending to Dawson Pass. Stay to the left. About 400 yards farther is the intersection with the trail that traverses around the south shore of Two Medicine Lake. You may elect to return to the foot of Two Medicine Lake via this route. However, the trail is not frequently maintained. Prepare to climb over several downfallen trees. As another option you may select to return to the foot of the lake by way of an excursion boat. If so, take this trail to the boat dock at the head of the lake. The boat operates during the busiest part of the tourist season. The concessionaire charges a fee.

Shortly after this trail junction you will arrive at the spur trail to Twin Falls. A sidetrip to this unique pair of waterfalls is recommended. Twin Falls is about 100 yards from the North Shore Trail. The falls are technically cascades but that makes them no less impressive. Wildflowers abound at the base and on both sides of the falls. Look for dippers feeding in the waters at the base of the falls and in the creek.

After Twin Falls the North Shore Trail winds through a mixed forest of subalpine fir, spruce, and Douglas fir trees. There are abundant displays of wildflowers in the open meadows below the rocky crags of Rising Wolf Mountain. To your left a small pond looks like it is set amid perfect moose habitat.

You are nearing Upper Two Medicine Lake when you walk onto a solid rock outcropping. This sill at the foot of the lake serves as a natural dam for the water of Two Medicine Creek.

Take a moment to survey the country you have walked over before you venture to the lake. Looking east from the sill will provide a panoramic view of the Two Medicine watershed and its characteristic U-shaped glacier-carved valley. Close your eyes and imagine the massive layers of ice that filled this valley 18,000 years ago. The evidence of the glaciation is all around you, from the rock rubble on the valley floor to the hanging valleys to the south, and of course the lakes, some of which are in depressions left by the weight of the ice.

As you approach the shoreline of Upper Two Medicine Lake you will recognize it as a typical cirque lake carved out of the surrounding mountains by the head of a glacier. The sheer cliffs of red argillite lining the lake are Pumpelly Pillar to the north, then counterclockwise, 8,536-foot Mount Helen, Lone Walker Mountain at 8,502 feet, and Mount Rockwell at 9,272 feet in elevation. Look for mountain goats on the ledges along the sheer cliff faces and next to the dark green forests of fir and spruce.

The Two Medicine Chalet

The Two Medicine Camp Store is the only remaining structure of the Two Medicine Chalet complex. The store was the main dining hall, built in 1915. Other buildings included a dormitory and cabins. Except for the main dining hall all of the other buildings were removed during the winter of 1953. The Two Medicine Camp Store was included on the list of the National Register of Historic Places in 1987. When it was still the dining hall, Two Medicine Camp Store was the site of a speech broadcast by President Franklin Roosevelt, August 5, 1934. The broadcast was not one of his official "Fireside Chats." In his speech President Roosevelt exclaimed, "Today for the first time in my life I have seen Glacier Park. Perhaps I can best express to you my thrill and delight by saying that I wish every American, both old and young, could have been with me today. The great mountains, the glacier, the lakes and the trees make me long to stay for the rest of the summer." He left early the next morning, having stayed less than 24 hours in the park.

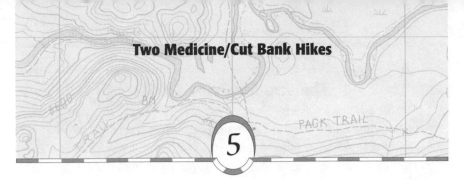

Appistoki Falls

This is a short and delightful walk through a young forest to a waterfall above a series of cataracts and turquoise pools.

Level of difficulty: Easy.

Distance: 1.2 miles round trip.

Duration: 1 hour.

Best time of year: June–September.

Trailhead: Appistoki Falls can be accessed by way of the Mount Henry Trailhead 0.25 mile east of Two Medicine Campground along Two Medicine Road.

Hiking directions: The sign at the trailhead designates the trail as the Mount Henry Trail. The trail begins narrow, relatively flat, and winding. At 0.6 mile you come to the Appistoki Falls Trail. The Appistoki Falls overlook is 200 feet along this spur trail.

Special attention: The viewpoint for Appistoki Falls is a sheer dropoff into a canyon. Special care should be taken at the overlook because there is not a guardrail. Children should be closely watched.

Notes: After leaving the parking lot you immediately enter a forest of subalpine firs, spruce trees, and lodgepole pines. The trail is easy to hike and well defined. A large number of hikers use this trail. Many of the hikers have Scenic Point as their destination. The understory is mostly beargrass (a lily) and various species of grasses. Watch for ruffed grouse and listen for nuthatches and chickadees.

Appistoki Creek drains the valley enclosed by three main landforms, Scenic Point to the east at 7,522 feet, Mount Henry to the south at 8,847 feet, and Appistoki Peak, with an elevation of 8,164 feet, to the west. The wind and weather in this valley can be harsh. You can catch sight of the windswept and open mountainside of Appistoki Peak from the waterfall viewpoint.

To the north, across the valley floor, is massive Rising Wolf Mountain. Rising Wolf is the Piegan Blackfeet name given to Hugh Monroe, a native of Quebec, Canada. An employee of the Hudson's Bay Company, Monroe relocated to

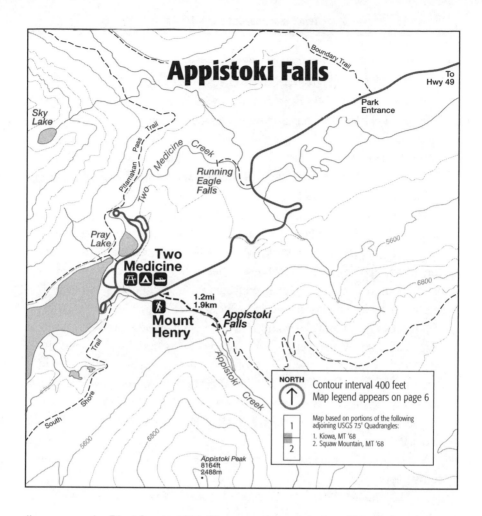

Appistoki Falls

live among the Blackfeet in 1814. He spent the remainder of his life hunting and trapping in the area around St. Mary. Sometime during the 1840s he was involved in a christening ceremony on the shore of the lower lake. He and his companions who attended the christening erected a cross and named the lake St. Mary.

Chickadees and Nuthatches

As you walk through fir-spruce forests you frequently will hear the easily imitated chick-a-dee song and the high-pitched calls of the chickadee. If you focus your attention on the direction from which the song comes you will likely notice that the chickadee is not alone. It is traveling in a flock that might include other species such as nuthatches, brown creepers, juncos, and downy woodpeckers.

The reasons for the different species flocking together is unclear, although several unconfirmed explanations exist. Perhaps it is for safety. Each species has a different way of reacting to predators. When the members of one species become frightened their actions alert the other species of the potential danger. Another explanation for the flocking behavior is that the diets of the birds are similar. One species may "inform" the others of a food source. Nuthatches and brown creepers illustrate this phenomenon. Both species feed on the same food—insects concealed around the edges of treebark. You will commonly find them feeding together. Yet in order not to compete with each other the nuthatch walks down the tree trunk feeding on insects under the top edges of the bark, while the brown creeper spirals up the tree trunk extracting the same insect species from under the bottom crevices of the bark.

When you hear the characteristic chick-a-dee song look for his traveling companions.

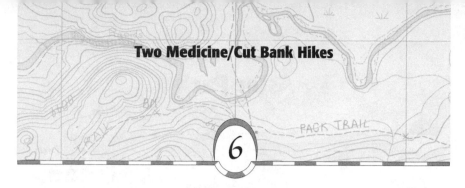

6

Aster Park

This short hike will lead you through an enchanting forest, to a lovely waterfall, and to an impressive panoramic view of the Two Medicine Valley.

Level of difficulty: Moderate.

Distance: 3.8 miles round trip.

Duration: 2–3 hours.

Best time of year: July–September.

Trailhead: The South Shore Trailhead is at the west end of the Two Medicine Lake parking area, next to the excursion boat dock.

Hiking directions: Follow the South Shore Trail until you cross Aster Creek on a footbridge. Then, follow the Aster Park Trail south to Aster Park.

Notes: The lower reaches of the trail offer a gradual ascent away from Two Medicine Lake through a subalpine forest of fir, spruce, and western larch. The trail is level and works inland through marshy areas and small meadows filled with wildflowers.

At 0.4 mile a well marked spur trail takes off to the right and will direct you to Paradise Point on the south shore of Two Medicine Lake. From this vantage point you will have a beautifully framed view of the awe-inspiring Rising Wolf Mountain to the north. At 9,513 feet in elevation it extends 4,349 feet above the valley floor.

Return to the South Shore Trail after taking in the beauty of Paradise Point. You will soon cross Aster Creek on a footbridge and find the Aster Park Trail on the other side. The Aster Park Trail begins a slow and direct climb through the forest of pine and fir until you reach the Aster Falls spur trail. The spur trail leads about 100 feet to the base of the cascading waterfall. Aster Creek has cut through the bedrock but finds ample resistance to produce this lovely water display.

Aster Park is an additional 0.7 mile above the waterfall. But before you can reach the park, you must switchback through the forest. This part of the trail is rated moderate in difficulty; the rest of the trail is relatively easy.

The trail ends at a rocky point overlooking Two Medicine Lake. Note the

many wasted remains of whitebark pine trees killed by the whitebark pine blister rust disease.

The landmark Sinopah Mountain dominates the view to the west. Rising Wolf Mountain looks just as large as it does from Paradise Point. Turning away from the lake you will be looking up the Aster Creek Valley. Precipitation falling on these mountains provides the source of water for Aster Creek. To the southwest you will see 7,641-foot Never Laughs Mountain; 8,581-foot Mount Ellsworth is to the south, and to the east is a flank of massive 8,847-foot Mount Henry. Notice the large open meadows on these mountainsides. There are no established trails into the Aster Creek Valley. This area is left solely to the resident plants and animals and the whispering wind.

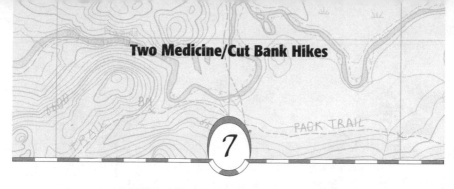

Medicine Grizzly Lake

Stunning waterfalls, cascades, and sheer cliff faces dominate the landscape at Medicine Grizzly Lake. This hike is the best choice for the traveler wanting to experience the Cut Bank environment of Glacier National Park.

Level of difficulty: Strenuous.

Distance: 13 miles round trip to the head of the lake.

Duration: 6–7 hours.

Best time of year: Late June–October.

Trailhead: The trailhead is at the backcountry parking site at the entrance to Cut Bank Campground. A sign identifies the trail as Pitamakan Pass Trail.

Hiking directions: The first part of the trail is an abandoned roadbed through a meadow and into the forest along the bank of the North Fork of Cut Bank Creek. Soon after entering the forest the trail splits. The segment to the left, along the creek, leads to the site of the Cut Bank Chalet, which was removed in 1949. The trail to Medicine Grizzly Lake is to the right.

Special attention: Snow can stay late in the forest along the North Fork of Cut Bank Creek. The trail can be muddy in areas throughout the summer months. This can pose some problems for hikers but presents an opportunity for you to look for wildlife tracks in the mud of the trail. Hiking to Medicine Grizzly Lake in late June or after August can minimize your contact with mosquitoes and biting flies.

Notes: The trail is narrow, provides good footing, and is well maintained. After leaving the creek the trail enters a mixed-age forest of spruce, Douglas fir, and pine. The damp conditions in the forest and along the trail offer the amateur mycologist a delightful experience. You will find several species of mushrooms growing along the trail throughout the summer and well into autumn.

The mountains to your immediate left are 8,341-foot Mad Wolf Mountain, and 8,360-foot Bad Marriage Mountain. Soon the trail breaks out of the forest about 100 feet above the creek. This gives you a good elevated view of the immediate watershed. When you enter the second meadow you will get an

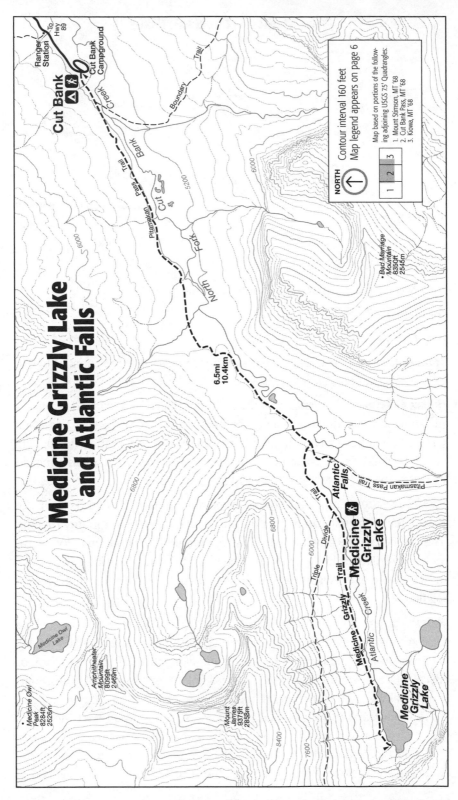

Medicine Grizzly Lake and Atlantic Falls

NORTH

Contour interval 160 feet
Map legend appears on page 6

Map based on portions of the following adjoining USGS 7.5' Quadrangles:
1. Mount Stimson, MT '68
2. Cut Bank Pass, MT '68
3. Kiowa, MT '68

Ranger Station
Cut Bank Campground
To Hwy 89

Cut Bank

Cut Bank Creek

Boundary Trail

Pitamakan Pass Trail

Cut C

5200

North Fork

6000

6000

6.5mi
10.4km

Bad Marriage Mountain
8350ft
2545m

Medicine Owl Peak
8284ft
2526m

Medicine Owl Lake

Amphitheater Mountain
8099ft
2469m

6800

6800

6000

Mount James
9375ft
2858m

Triple Divide Trail

Atlantic Falls Trail

Pitamakan Pass Trail

Medicine Grizzly Lake

Medicine Grizzly Trail

Atlantic Creek

8400

7600

Medicine Grizzly Lake

excellent view of the mountains to the north. To your immediate right is the massive 8,797-foot Kupunkamint Mountain, and in front of you is Amphitheater Mountain at 8,690 feet.

The trail alternately passes through meadows, open forests, and deep forests. The meadows have many wildflowers throughout the warm months. Among the myriad wildflower species expect to find paintbrush, asters, goldenrod, lupine, fireweed, beargrass, kinnikinnick, huckleberry, harebell, cinquefoil, sticky geranium, and cow parsnips. The forested areas are mostly composed of lodgepole pine, willow thickets, aspen groves, alder, and black cottonwood. You will hear chickadees and nuthatches calling in the forest as they move from pine tree to pine tree selecting seeds and insects to eat.

At 2 miles you come to a wide creekbed. This broad wash carries runoff from the valley between Kupunkamint Mountain and Amphitheater Mountain. A healthy stand of mature black cottonwood trees can be seen in the lower reaches of the wash. You can detect in the air the characteristic fragrance of the cottonwood species. Soon after leaving the wash you will be able to see 7,397-foot Triple Divide Peak in front of you to your right. Directly in front of you is Razoredge Mountain.

At the 3 mile mark the trail passes a 5-acre unnamed pond adjacent to the North Fork of Cut Bank Creek. At 3.9 miles you will come to the junction of Triple Divide Pass Trail and Pitamakan Pass Trail. Take the Pitamakan Pass Trail for the next quarter of a mile to Atlantic Creek. The trail passes over a footbridge below Atlantic Falls. The falls are comprised of several ledges with many species of wildflowers blooming on and around the ledges.

Backtrack to Triple Divide Pass Trail to continue your quest for Medicine Grizzly Lake. The trail begins to climb through an open-mature mixed forest of subalpine fir, Douglas fir, and spruce. At 0.5 mile from the trail junction is the Atlantic Creek backcountry campground. After another 0.3 mile you come to a trail junction to Medicine Grizzly Lake and Triple Divide Pass. The trail remains a narrow winding path with splendid stands of beargrass. During late summer the trail is almost overgrown. The last 2 miles are through forest and large meadows filled with beargrass and fireweed. The large peak in front of you and to your right is Triple Divide Peak with Triple Divide Pass to the immediate right of the peak. Large snowfields feed the cascades coming from the Peak and Razoredge Mountain.

The view of moderately sized Medicine Grizzly Lake from the foot of the lake is spectacular with the headwalls, cascades, and looming peaks. The trail continues along the northern shoreline to the head of the lake where you can view and listen to the long and sinuous cascades up close.

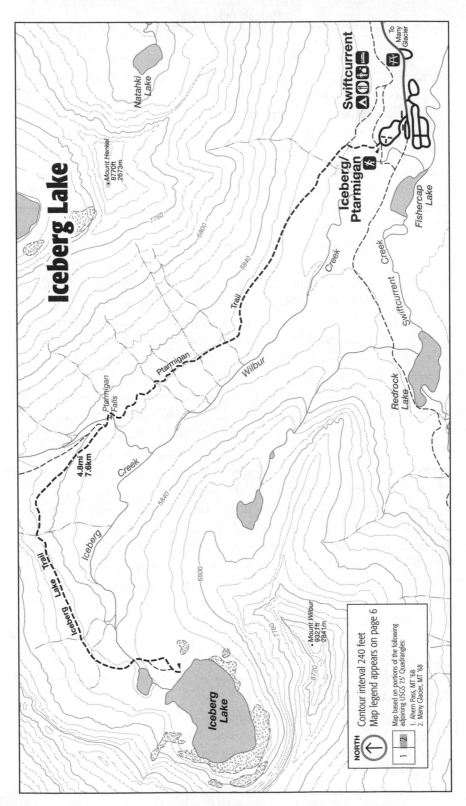

Iceberg Lake

Natahki Lake

Mount Henkel
8770ft
2673m

Swiftcurrent

To Many Glacier

Iceberg/Ptarmigan

Fishercap Lake

Ptarmigan Trail

Ptarmigan Falls

Wilbur Creek

Swiftcurrent Creek

Redrock Lake

4.8mi
7.6km

Iceberg Creek

Iceberg Lake Trail

Mount Wilbur
9321ft
2841m

Iceberg Lake

NORTH

Contour interval 240 feet
Map legend appears on page 6

Map based on portions of the following
adjoining USGS 7.5' Quadrangles:

1. Ahern Pass, MT '68
2. Many Glacier, MT '68

34

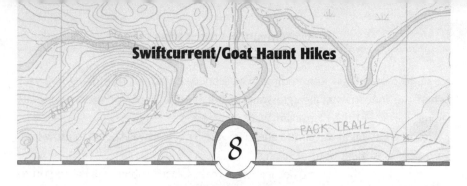

8

Iceberg Lake

The walk to Iceberg Lake is through an alpine area fed all summer by melting snow and glaciers. The walk provides a vast panorama of fantastic beauty.

Level of difficulty: Moderate.

Distance: 9.5 miles round trip.

Duration: 5–6 hours.

Best time of year: July–August.

Trailhead: The trail begins at the western end of the Swiftcurrent Motor Inn parking lot off Many Glacier Road. The trailhead sign reads "Swiftcurrent Pass."

Hiking directions: Look for the trailhead sign that reads "Swiftcurrent Pass" at the end of the parking lot. Continue on this trail a short distance and then follow the signs for the Ptarmigan Trail.

Special attention: This trail may be closed at various times in order to allow grizzly bears to roam without intrusion.

Notes: The trail skirts the western flank of 8,770-foot Mount Henkel and climbs through patches of aspen trees and lodgepole pines and through meadows. The meadows are filled with alpine wildflowers including paintbrush, glacier lilies, and asters, as well as fireweed, beargrass, and wild roses, depending on the season. The understory is mostly serviceberry, buffaloberry, snowberry, and huckleberry bushes.

Along the way you will be viewing the Ptarmigan Wall in front of you. You can see the Iceberg Lake Trail as it crosses the Wall. To your left is massive Mount Wilbur. The trail climbs nearly 700 feet above Wilbur Creek in the next 2.5 miles. At this point the trail crosses Ptarmigan Creek on a footbridge above the steplike Ptarmigan Falls. A few hundred feet beyond the waterfall is a trail division. Stay left for Iceberg Lake. The right branch goes to Ptarmigan Lake, the Ptarmigan Tunnel, and the Belly River drainage.

From here the trail swings to the west and cuts across the lower reaches of the Ptarmigan Wall. Expect to climb another 500 feet in elevation in the next 2.2 miles. Iceberg Creek is far below you. This increase in elevation will take you into more alpine surroundings. The scenery is particularly striking in a year when the meadows of beargrass are in full bloom. Look for mountain goats along the face of the Ptarmigan Wall.

Iceberg Lake is in the cirque ahead of you. The headwall seems to grow larger during your next hour of hiking.

At 4.4 miles the trail crosses Iceberg Creek. Glacial rubble will cause you to climb and then descend for the next 0.3 mile. As you climb, you will cross meadows crowded with breathtakingly beautiful alpine wildflowers and walk through patches of low-growing subalpine fir trees. A picturesque small, unnamed tarn lies in a flowery meadow a few hundred feet below Iceberg Lake.

Appropriately named, Iceberg Lake will stay frozen until late spring and have small icebergs floating in its cold water well into the summer season. The lake stays cold because it is at nearly 6,100 feet in elevation and tucked away in a northeast-facing cirque. Therefore, it receives little direct sunlight during the year. The melting snowfields and receding glaciers supply the glacial flour that gives the water its milky-blue shade.

Swiftcurrent Lake Loop

This is a wonderful walk for visitors to Glacier who are not inclined to pursue a challenging hike. A stroll around the lake after a long day of sightseeing by car is a good way to unwind and develop an intimate appreciation of the Many Glacier area.

Level of difficulty: Easy.

Distance: 2.6 miles.

Duration: 2–3 hours.

Best time of year: June–October.

Trailhead: There are two access points to the Swiftcurrent Lake Trail. One trailhead is off the parking lot of the picnic area of the Grinnell Lake Trail, 0.5 mile west of the turnoff to Many Glacier Hotel on Many Glacier Road. The second access is near the shoreline of Swiftcurrent Lake at the southern end of Many Glacier Hotel.

Hiking directions: You can begin your walk at either trailhead. Halfway around Swiftcurrent Lake you will encounter the Grinnell Glacier Trail junction. Walk 0.2 mile along this trail to see picturesque Lake Josephine. The trail is paved and highly recommended due to the beauty of the lake.

Special attention: This is bear and moose country. Even on a warm summer day, with many visitors using the trail, you could be surprised by either animal walking out of the deep understory onto the trail.

Notes: This is a self-guided nature trail. The National Park Service has provided pamphlets that can be acquired for 50 cents at both trailheads The pamphlets do not specify stops along the trail but are a running commentary on the natural history of the Swiftcurrent Lake area. Acquiring the pamphlet is advised.

The forest you are walking through includes subalpine fir, lodgepole pine, spruce, and aspen trees. The verdant understory includes snowberry, serviceberry, thimbleberry, queencup, and aster, as well as countless ferns and mushrooms.

You will be serenaded by nuthatches and chickadees as they fly from tree to

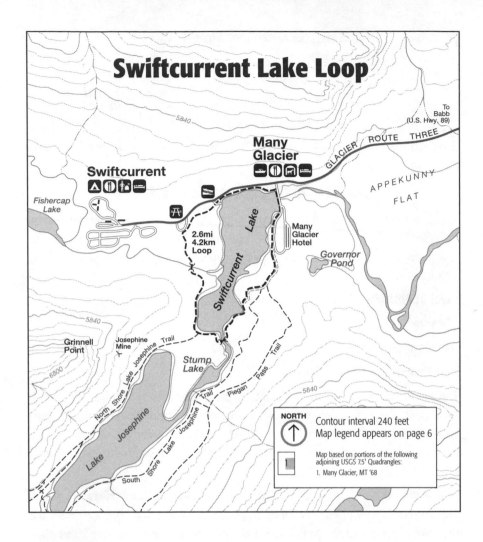

Swiftcurrent Lake Loop

To Babb (U.S. Hwy. 89)

GLACIER ROUTE THREE

APPEKUNNY FLAT

Many Glacier

Swiftcurrent

Fishercap Lake

2.6mi 4.2km Loop

Many Glacier Hotel

Governor Pond

Swiftcurrent Lake

Grinnell Point

Josephine Mine

Josephine Trail

Stump Lake

Piegan Pass Trail

North Shore Lake Josephine Trail

Lake Josephine

South Shore Lake Josephine Trail

NORTH

Contour interval 240 feet
Map legend appears on page 6

Map based on portions of the following adjoining USGS 7.5' Quadrangles:
1. Many Glacier, MT '68

tree, eating seeds and insects while you walk around the lake enjoying the magnificent sights. Regardless of where you are on the lakeshore you will have wonderful views of the water, the Swiftcurrent Valley, the Grinnell Valley, Grinnell Point, 9,376-foot Allen Mountain, 9,321-foot Mount Wilbur, and Altyn Peak. Altyn Peak was formerly known as Crow Feet Mountain for the last chief of the Blackfeet confederacy of tribes.

The short walk to Lake Josephine will bring you to a boat ramp. From this vantage point you can view a lake that is about the size of Swiftcurrent Lake. Lake Josephine is bounded by Grinnell Peak, 8,851-foot Mount Grinnell, and Allen Mountain. Look to your right, on the side of Grinnell Peak, and you will see evidence of the mining efforts in Grinnell Valley at the Josephine Mine. Long abandoned, the mine is a reminder of efforts to extract riches from the Glacier area before it was established as a national park in 1910.

Grinnell Valley

Once referred to as Land of the Walled-in Lakes by Blackfeet Indians, the lush, wild, rocky Grinnell Valley has myriad wonders. Plan to spend at least a day exploring the area.

Level of difficulty: Easy.

Distance: 13 miles round trip.

Duration: 8 hours.

Best time of year: Late June–October.

Trailhead: The trailhead is off the parking lot 0.5 mile west of Many Glacier Hotel on Many Glacier Road. The trailhead is marked as "Grinnell Glacier Trailhead."

Hiking directions: Begin your walk on the Swiftcurrent Lake Trail. Walk around the western shore of Swiftcurrent Lake to the trail junction to Grinnell Lake. The next 0.2 mile is on a paved trail to Lake Josephine. When you reach the boat landing at Lake Josephine look on the slope of the mountain to your right. Several hundred feet above the lake on the side of Grinnell Point is evidence of attempts to extract precious ore from this area. The holes in the side of the mountain are part of the abandoned Josephine Mine. Continue around the western shore of Lake Josephine. At the head of Lake Josephine you will come to a trail divide; to the right is access to an overlook of Grinnell Glacier. To the left is the valley floor. Take the trail to the left in order to explore the valley floor. At the head of the lake you cross Cataract Creek on a footbridge and swampy areas on a boardwalk. After you leave the boardwalk, the trail turns to the right, up the valley. Upon your return, you may wish to stay on the eastern side of Lake Josephine. The eastern trail, used by outfitters from the hotel concession, takes you to the vicinity of the boat dock at the head of Swiftcurrent Lake.

Special attention: The Grinnell Valley is prime moose and bear country. Be aware that you are a visitor in their territory. Both animals can be unpredictable and should be regarded as potentially dangerous.

Notes: There are several prominent features in the Grinnell Valley you should

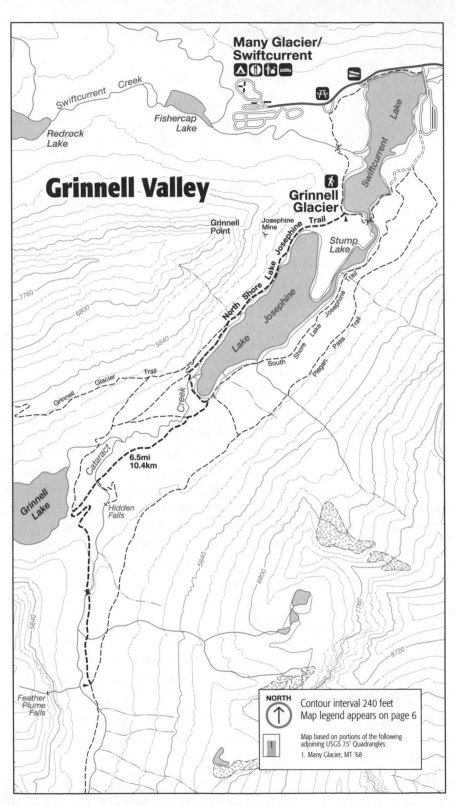

Many Glacier/
Swiftcurrent

Swiftcurrent Creek

Fishercap
Lake

Redrock
Lake

Swiftcurrent Lake

Grinnell Valley

Grinnell Glacier

Grinnell
Point

Josephine Trail

Josephine
Mine

Stump
Lake

North Shore Lake Josephine

Lake Josephine

South Shore Lake Josephine Trail

Piegan Pass Trail

Grinnell Glacier Trail

Creek

Cataract

**6.5mi
10.4km**

Grinnell
Lake

Hidden
Falls

7760

6800

5840

5840

6800

7760

8720

Feather
Plume
Falls

5840

NORTH

Contour interval 240 feet
Map legend appears on page 6

1

Map based on portions of the following
adjoining USGS 7.5' Quadrangles:
1. Many Glacier, MT '68

consider exploring, including Grinnell Lake, Feather Plume Falls, Lake Josephine, Hidden Falls, Cataract Creek, and the forest and meadow wildflowers.

The western flank of Grinnell Peak is awash with the colors of wildflowers throughout the growing season. Expect to find serviceberry, elderberry, harebell, mountain aster, snowberry, pearlyeverlasting, and huckleberry. Trees growing on this mountainside include juniper, maple, Douglas fir, spruce, and subalpine fir. Birds that you will commonly find feeding and nesting in this area are nuthatches, robins, juncos, and chickadees.

Cataract Creek is aptly named. It is a swift-moving body of water that tumbles over rocks, sometimes outside its bank, flooding lowlands. Look for elk, moose, deer, and bear tracks in the mud.

Hidden Falls is a series of waterfalls, cascades, and pools tucked away into a narrow cleft. It is impressive how the water has cut through the weak rock layer to establish the falls. The color of the water contrasted with the rock is equally impressive. The mountain peak framed by the trees around the falls is a shoulder of Mount Gould known as Angel Wing.

Grinnell Lake is a medium-sized alpine lake at the foot of Grinnell Falls and the Grinnell Glacier. Parts of the Grinnell Glacier, the largest glacier in the park, can be seen at the head of the valley.

Feather Plume Falls is located an additional 1.2 miles from Grinnell Lake along the Feather Plume Cutoff Trail. It has a long misty appearance that makes it worthy of its lyrical name.

During the height of the visitor season, a boat tour is available from Many Glacier Hotel to the head of Swiftcurrent Lake and from the foot of Lake Josephine to the head of the lake. A fee is charged. About 4 miles can be cut off your hike by using the boat cruise.

George Bird Grinnell

Every national park has at least one person who championed the cause and carried the vision of national park designation to reality. John Muir is associated with Yosemite National Park. Enos Mills fought for the establishment of Rocky Mountain National Park. The person who is regarded as spearheading the inclusion of Glacier in the national park system is George Bird Grinnell. For his efforts the Boone and Crockett Club gave him the title Father of Glacier National Park.

During his 89 years Grinnell had many experiences—any one of which would satisfy the adventurous spirit of most people. As a young boy George Bird Grinnell attended school at his neighbor's house, the home of John James Audubon. It was at this time that he developed a love for birds and natural history. This interest in natural history lead him to earn two degrees in the field from Yale University.

As a respected natural history authority Grinnell was invited to serve as a naturalist on George Armstrong Custer's expedition to the Black Hills in 1874. Custer was so impressed with his work that he asked Grinnell to accompany him as a naturalist on his 1876 expedition. Fortuitously, Grinnell declined because of his duties at the Peabody Museum in New Haven, Connecticut. This second expedition ended with the Battle of the Little Bighorn.

In 1880, Grinnell became the editor-in-chief of *Forest and Stream* magazine. Stories submitted to the magazine by James Willard Schultz, a white man living among the Blackfeet, encouraged Grinnell to visit the northern Rocky Mountains. In 1885 he made his first of several trips to what was to become Glacier National Park. It was during this time that Grinnell founded the Audubon Society of New York, forerunner of the National Audubon Society. Along with then-Congressman Theodore Roosevelt, Grinnell became a founding member of the Boone and Crockett Club in 1887. Grinnell began to write in *Forest and Stream* about the area he called the "crown of the continent" and used his political contacts to encourage preservation of the Glacier area. His efforts were rewarded when Glacier became a national park in 1910.

Swiftcurrent Valley

Lakes, waterfalls, wildflowers, and wildlife are abundant in the Swiftcurrent Valley. Most visitors could easily spend a day exploring this east slope watershed. Don't forget your camera, wildflower identification book, and lunch.

Level of difficulty: Easy.

Distance: 17 miles round trip.

Duration: 7–8 hours.

Best time of year: July–September.

Trailhead: The trail begins at the western end of the Swiftcurrent Motor Inn parking lot off Many Glacier Road.

Hiking directions: Look for the trailhead sign that reads "Swiftcurrent Pass" and take that trail. You are now on the Continental Divide Trail, a National Scenic Trail that extends from Canada to Mexico. Unlike the Grinnell Valley, there is only one trail through the Swiftcurrent Valley.

Special attention: This trail may be closed part of the summer season due to the needs of resident bears.

Notes: This walk will take you along Swiftcurrent Creek with its numerous cascades and waterfalls—the most notable being Redrock Falls—and past three medium-sized lakes. Each lake is worthy of exploration.

The three lakes are almost identical in size. The first lake you come to is Fishercap Lake. It is about 100 feet off the main trail and is marked with a sign. The lake is surrounded by forest of lodgepole pine, aspen, and willow. The north side of Grinnell Peak and Grinnell Mountain loom over Fishercap Lake as well as the whole southern half of the valley.

From Fishercap Lake the trail begins a slow climb through a lodgepole pine and aspen forest while skirting the southern base of Mount Wilbur. This 9,321-foot mass was given the name Heavy Shield Mountain by the Blackfeet. The forest you are walking through has a healthy understory of wild roses, aster, snowberry, beargrass, paintbrush, and thimbleberry.

At 2 miles the trail reaches the foot of Redrock Lake. Your attention may be

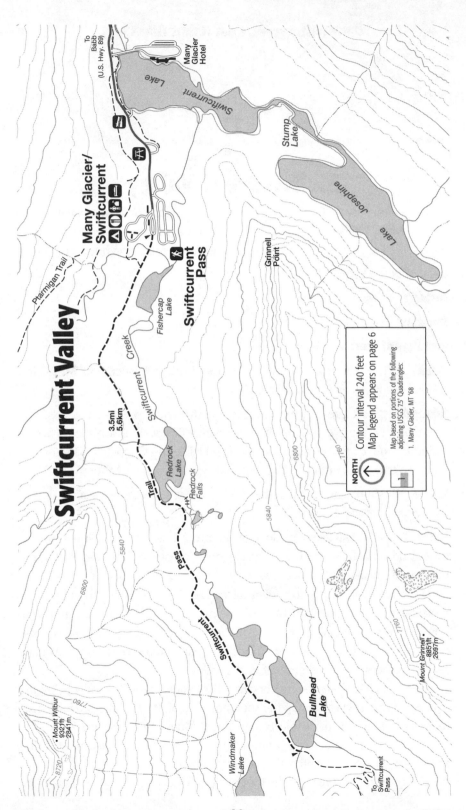

Swiftcurrent Valley

Many Glacier/ Swiftcurrent

Swiftcurrent Pass

To Babb
(U.S. Hwy. 89)

Many Glacier Hotel

Swiftcurrent Lake

Stump Lake

Lake Josephine

Grinnell Point

Ptarmigan Trail

Fishercap Lake

Swiftcurrent Creek

3.5mi
5.6km

Redrock Lake

Redrock Falls

Pass

Swiftcurrent Trail

Swiftcurrent

Bullhead Lake

Windmaker Lake

Mount Wilbur
9321ft
2841m

Mount Grinnell
8851ft
2697m

To Swiftcurrent Pass

6800

5840

5840

6800

8720

7760

7760

1760

6800

1760

NORTH

Contour interval 240 feet
Map legend appears on page 6

Map based on portions of the following
adjoining USGS 7.5' Quadrangles:

1. Many Glacier, MT '68

drawn toward the head of the lake, however, by the sound of roaring water from Redrock Falls. Redrock Falls is a series of waterfalls and pools that rush over eroded argillite rock. As you make your way around the lake notice the low-growing aspens and pines. These trees, affected by the wind, grow next to to Redrock Falls.

It is not possible to see the entire waterfall series from one vantage point. You will need to explore the area by accessing the creek bank by several short side trails. Each access point will provide you with wonderful views of the clear, foaming water swirling and rushing over deeply colored red rock. There are several good vantage points for waterfall photography. The main trail arrives at the head of the waterfall series to provide you with a view of a smooth-flowing, almost placid, stream. This view is in contrast to the scene to your left as gravity pulls the water crashing over rocks on its way to Redrock Lake.

The trail continues west for another 1.5 miles to Bullhead Lake. The glacier perched high on the wall at the end of the lake is Swiftcurrent Glacier. On the western side of the headwall is the Granite Park Chalet. The chalet can be accessed by a rigorous climb along the trail you are currently walking.

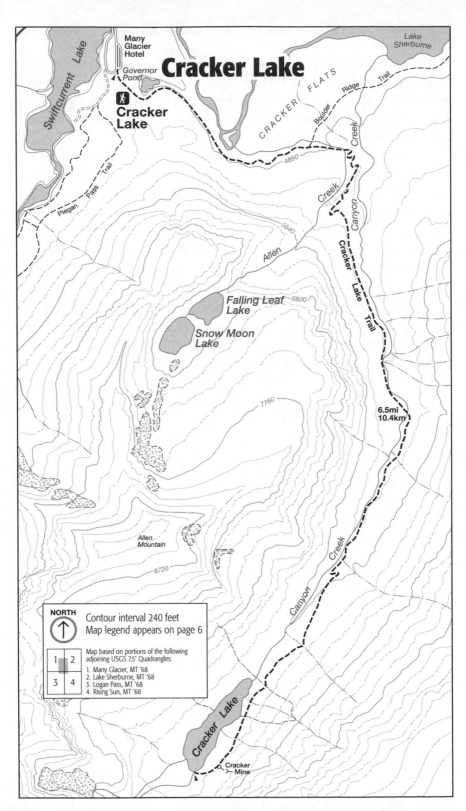

Cracker Lake

Swiftcurrent Lake

Many Glacier Hotel

Governor Pond

Cracker Lake

Lake Sherburne

CRACKER FLATS

Boulder Ridge Trail

Creek

Canyon

Creek

Piegan Pass Trail

4880

5840

Allen

Falling Leaf Lake

6800

Snow Moon Lake

Cracker Lake Trail

7760

6.5mi
10.4km

Allen Mountain

8720

Canyon Creek

Canyon

Cracker Lake

Cracker Mine

NORTH

Contour interval 240 feet
Map legend appears on page 6

1	2
3	4

Map based on portions of the following
adjoining USGS 7.5' Quadrangles:

1. Many Glacier, MT '68
2. Lake Sherburne, MT '68
3. Logan Pass, MT '68
4. Rising Sun, MT '68

Cracker Lake

Cracker Lake is one of the preeminent destinations in Glacier National Park. The hike to this striking alpine lake leads you through stunning montane and subalpine forests. This is a long day hike that is well worth your effort.

Level of difficulty: Strenuous.

Distance: 13 miles round trip.

Duration: 6–7 hours.

Best time of year: July–September.

Trailhead: The trailhead is at the south end of the parking area for the Many Glacier Hotel. The trailhead sign reads "Cracker Lake, Piegan Pass."

Hiking directions: Follow the Cracker Lake Trail to Cracker Lake. There will be places where the trail splits due to equestrians taking alternative routes. At 1.3 miles you encounter the junction with Cracker Flats Horse Trail. Continue to the right. It is at Cracker Flats that the mining town of Altyn was located. The townsite was inundated by water with the establishment of Lake Sherburne.

Special attention: Hikers and packers use the Cracker Lake Trail. Give horses the right-of-way by standing on the downhill side of the trail.

Notes: The trail begins in a mixed forest of aspen, whitebark pine, subalpine fir, and Douglas fir, with an understory of buffaloberry, beargrass, cinquefoil, asters, junipers, snowberry, and thimbleberry. The trail breaks out of the forest in the first mile and passes above the head of Lake Sherburne, historically called Fighting Bears' Lake by the Blackfeet. Depending on the time of year this part of the lake will be either covered with shallow water or dry.

Soon after leaving the horse trail to Cracker Flats you will cross Allen Creek and begin an ascent through a thickly forested ridge between Allen Creek and Canyon Creek. Notice the contrast between the two creeks. The Allen Creek drainage is forested down to the water. The Canyon Creek drainage is actively eroding the creek bank. The direction of flow and cutting action of creeks is dependent on the rock layers below the surface. The Allen Creek rock layers are more resistant to erosion than the Canyon Creek rock layers.

The trail follows the crest of the ridge for a short distance then slowly makes its way into the Canyon Creek drainage. As the trail descends to the creekbed it crosses a small talus slope. This is a good place to observe the lichens growing on the rock fragments. Lichens are pioneer plants that break down the rocks with the acids they exude. The tiny cracks they form in the rocks fill with blown dust and the decaying lichens to provide soil for higher-order plants to take root.

The trail meets the rushing Canyon Creek and a footbridge has been provided for access to the opposite bank. From here the trail begins a long gentle climb toward your destination.

Within a mile after the footbridge the trail has a switchback. At this point you are afforded a view of the end of Canyon Creek Valley and the area of Cracker Lake. The lake is still more than a mile away. The trail will break out onto the slopes of Cracker Mountain and continue its climb, giving you views of the headwall of Mount Siyeh. Look for hoary marmots foraging for food in the rocky soil from here to the lake.

Just as the headwall is looming high, you come to a hill overlooking Cracker Lake. The striking beauty of the scene may startle the first-time visitor. The lake is deep turquoise because of sunlight refracting through glacial milk from the Siyeh Glacier in the water. Red argillite cliffs surrounding the lake on three sides contrast with the milky blue color of the lake. The Siyeh Glacier clinging to the shear towering north side of Mount Siyeh at the head of the lake is an imposing sight. The fourth side of the walled-in lake, the direction from which you hiked, has a commanding view of the glaciated valley with 8,655-foot Yellow Mountain 12 miles distant. Yellow Mountain is also known as Yellow Wolf Mountain for a warrior of the Small Robes Clan of the Pikuni Blackfeet tribe.

Attempts to extract precious metal ore from the area is evidenced by the tailings and shaft of the long-abandoned Cracker Mine on your left, on the west-facing slope of Cracker Mountain. In addition to the tailings and the mineshaft, a jumble of unused lead mining equipment is discarded at the head of the lake. The mining equipment is incongruent in the environment of the beautiful lake and mountains but adds an interesting historical twist to the essence of the glaciated valley.

The Cracker Lake area is hard to leave. You may be captivated for hours by the innumerable waterfalls around the lake. The backcountry campsites at the head of the lake may entice you to return for an extended visit.

Unused lead mining equipment at the head of Cracker Lake.

Mining in Glacier

Native Americans have lived in the Glacier area for thousands of years. Anglo-European presence is relatively recent. It is the white influence that has altered the landscape most dramatically. The first known white man to view the Glacier region was British explorer David Thompson during the 1780s. Westward expansion and the glory of discovery brought increasing numbers of adventurers. Most of these explorers left little record of their time in what is now Glacier National Park. From the 1820s to the 1850s fur trappers overran the region. Except for tall tales and a few fiscal accounting records the Glacier region remained mysterious. It wasn't until expeditions entered the area in order to map the region to establish an international boundary with Canada that accurate records were kept. Survey expeditions and increasingly easy access to the area influenced the timber and mineral exploiters to look for instant riches among the region's many resources. Between 1860 and 1910 timbermen, oilmen, and miners attempted to extract wealth from this mountainous region.

Most of the mining efforts centered on the Swiftcurrent Valley. Mines were dug, and communities were established. The mining community of Altyn proclaimed in its 1900, Volume 1, Number 1 newspaper, *The Swift Current Courier:* "Copper is King! No Doubt Now About the Permanency and Productiveness of the Swift Current Mines. The Growth of Altyn Now Assured."

The dream wasn't fulfilled. The ore was not high grade. The miners left, along with the oilmen and timbermen. However, the miners left behind part of their legacy. Some of the building foundations of Altyn can be seen on Cracker Flats when the level of Lake Sherburne drops, the Josephine Mine is visible above Lake Josephine on the side of Grinnell Peak, and mining debris sits at the head of Cracker Lake.

13

Appekunny Falls

This trail provides access to a long ribbon of water that cascades from Natahki Lake situated in a cirque at the eastern base of 8,770-foot Mount Henkel, formerly called Red Sore Eyes Mountain by the Blackfeet. It is a short but moderately difficult hike to this captivating place.

Level of difficulty: Moderate.

Distance: 2 miles round trip.

Duration: 1–2 hours.

Best time of year: June–October.

Trailhead: The trailhead is 3.3 miles west of the park entrance on Many Glacier Road. The parking area is on the north side of the road, distinguished by a large sign that reads "Poia Lake Hiking Trail." To the left of that sign is a trailhead sign indicating "Appekunny Falls Trail."

Hiking directions: Appekunny Falls Trail leads only to the waterfall.

Special attention: This trail is short, yet the last 0.5 mile requires that you climb over rocks to reach the base or the overlook of the waterfall.

Notes: The trail begins in a meadow dominated by fireweed, goldenrod, wild rose, serviceberry, beargrass, harebell, asters, buffaloberry, snowberry, thimbleberry, and wild strawberry. Aspen, subalpine fir, Douglas fir, whitebark pine, and spruce are the tree species you will encounter along the hike. After you leave the meadow you will begin to climb through the forest. The climb is steady and over many loose rocks. You will see the waterfall long before you reach it. The last 100 yards before the base of the waterfall or an overlook of the waterfall will be over large broken rocks. The trails are hard to follow.

As you look down the valley from the base of the falls you are looking at 8,404-foot Wynn Mountain and at Cracker Flats. It is on Cracker Flats that the town of Altyn was located until it was abandoned, and Lake Sherburne was allowed to flood the townsite. The only remnants of the community are the building foundations, apparent when the lake is low, and an unmarked gravesite

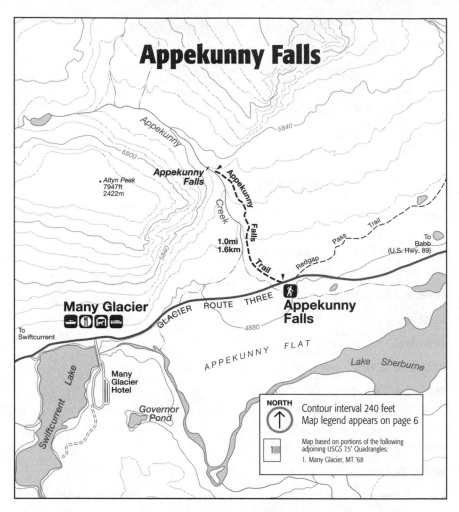

200 yards west of the Appekunny Falls Trailhead on the Many Glacier Road. The gravesite is distinguished by a low rock wall near a lone tree. There are various stories about who is buried at the site.

James Willard Shultz

The word Appekunny means "Far Off White Robe" in the Piegan Blackfeet language. The word has two spellings, Appekunny for the geologic rock formation and Apikuni for the mountain. Both spellings are correct; Blackfeet words historically have been spelled phonetically.

The name Appekunny was given to James Willard Schultz, a white man who moved from New York at the age of 17 to work at the Fort Conrad Trading Post. He married a Piegan woman and began living among the Blackfeet.

Schultz wrote about his life with the Blackfeet in the northern Rocky Mountains. He sent the stories to eastern publications. In 1885, an article he wrote was published in *Forest and Stream*. This article influenced the magazine's editor, George Bird Grinnell, to travel to the northern Rocky Mountains to investigate the region. Grinnell was so impressed with the area that he undertook to safeguard the region in the form of a national park. His publishing and political efforts were largely responsible for Glacier being designated as a national park in 1910. As a result of his work the Boone and Crocket Club bestowed on him the title of Father of Glacier National Park.

James Willard Schultz authored 20 books in addition to his prolific magazine contributions. Although most of his books are out of print, many are available via the World Wide Web and at used bookstores. You will find several of his books at retail outlets in and around the park. Among his most notable books in print are *Blackfeet Tales of Glacier Park; Bird Woman: Sacagawea's Own Story; My Life As an Indian; Blackfeet and Buffalo: Memories of Life Among the Indians; Blackfeet Tales from Apikuni's World;* and *With the Indians in the Rockies.*

14

Rainbow Falls

The walk to Rainbow Falls is a popular and easy stroll. Several people who arrive at Goat Haunt by way of the excursion boat from Waterton Township choose to take this walk and return to the township on a later boat.

Level of difficulty: Easy.

Distance: 2 miles round trip.

Duration: 1–2 hours.

Best time of year: June–September.

Trailhead: From the boat landing at Goat Haunt walk the 0.25-mile trail to the Goat Haunt ranger station. Look for the "Waterton Lake Trail" sign behind the ranger station. This is the trailhead for Rainbow Falls.

Hiking directions: You will reach the Waterton River after 0.25 mile. Soon after, you come to a trail junction; take the left option to Rainbow Falls.

Special attention: Inquire with the boat concessionaire personnel to ensure room will be available for you on a later return trip to Waterton Township. The trail ends at the top of the waterfall. Do not proceed farther.

Notes: The trail is relatively flat, 2 feet wide, and provides soft footing. You will be passing through the lower reaches of the Waterton River watershed. The forest is a characteristic mountain riparian zone with subalpine fir, Douglas fir, and maple trees. The mixed forest canopy allows a lot of sunlight to reach the forest floor, which supports a diverse and dense understory of snowberry, bracken ferns, and mosses. The trail is often lined by beargrass. The forest floor has a bountiful wildflower display during the summer and autumn.

You will soon approach a marshy area on your left. This is a seasonal pond and wetland containing enough mineral deposits to attract animals to drink the enriched water. These areas are sometimes referred to as mineral licks, or salt licks.

After taking you around the wetland, the trail will veer left and you'll begin a short climb through a young lodgepole pine forest. The trail takes a tight righthand bend and terminates at the top of Rainbow Falls, which can be

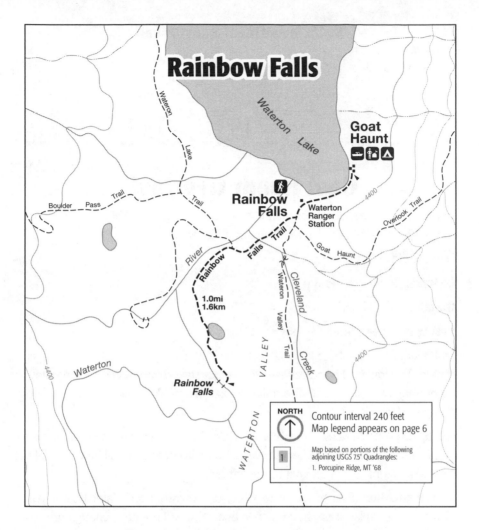

described as a cascade or a cataract. There are a number of beautiful lucent pools within the cataract. The top of the waterfall is a pleasant spot to have a snack, listen to the cascading water, and look for dippers along the creek.

Goat Haunt Overlook

The Overlook provides a panoramic view of the Waterton Valley wherein lies the border between the United States and Canada.

Level of difficulty: Moderate.

Distance: 2 miles round trip.

Duration: 1–2 hours.

Best time of year: June–September.

Trailhead: From the boat landing, walk the 0.25-mile paved trail to the ranger station. The trailhead is located past the ranger station and beyond the employee housing at Goat Haunt. The trailhead sign reads "Waterton Valley Trail and Waterton Lake Trail."

Hiking directions: Follow the Waterton Valley Trail, which has been designated as a National Scenic Trail. After 100 yards you will come to a trail junction. Take the Goat Haunt Overlook Trail to the left.

Special attention: Plan to return to Waterton Township on a later boat if you arrived at Goat Haunt on the excursion boat. You will not have enough time to walk to Goat Haunt Overlook and return on the same boat. Inquire with the boat concessionaire personnel to ensure room will be available for you on a later return trip to Waterton Township.

Notes: The trail to Goat Haunt Overlook is a narrow pathway with good footing that climbs from lake level to 800 feet above the lake in about 1 mile. The trail climbs steadily through the forest. At the 0.75 mile mark, the forest becomes more dense with Douglas fir, subalpine fir, lodgepole pine, juniper, aspens, and maples. The lush understory has healthy growth of thimbleberry, fireweed, beargrass, serviceberry, pearlyeverlasting, wild onion, kinnikinnick, harebell, daisies, asters, paintbrush, sticky geranium, coneflowers, and cinquefoil. The trail breaks out into meadows three times before reaching the overlook. The end of the trail is marked with a sign.

The Overlook affords a commanding panoramic view of the south end of Waterton Lake (named after eighteenth century British naturalist Charles

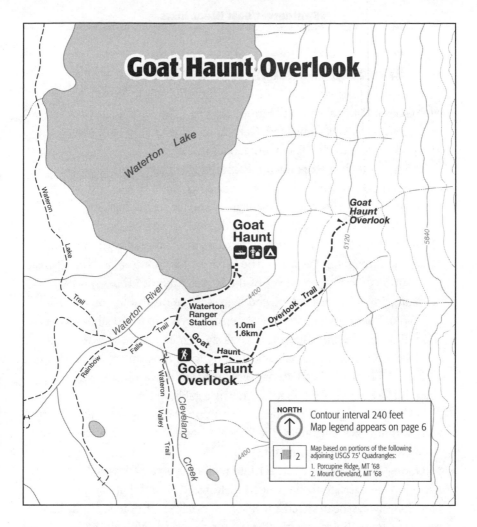

Goat Haunt Overlook

Waterton Lake

Waterton

Lake

Trail

Waterton River

Falls

Trail

Rainbow

Goat
Haunt

Waterton
Ranger
Station

Goat
Haunt

Goat Haunt
Overlook

Waterton

Cleveland

Valley

Trail

Creek

Goat
Haunt
Overlook

Overlook Trail

5120

5640

1.0mi
1.6km

4400

4400

NORTH

Contour interval 240 feet
Map legend appears on page 6

2

Map based on portions of the following
adjoining USGS 7.5' Quadrangles:
1. Porcupine Ridge, MT '68
2. Mount Cleveland, MT '68

Waterton); the 7,750-foot Citadel Peaks to the southeast, 7,913-foot Olson Mountain directly across the lake, and the tallest mountain you can see to the west, Campbell Mountain rising to 8,245 feet. The stately Prince of Wales Hotel can be seen far to the north.

Somewhere to the north of where you are standing, running through the forest and across the lake, is an undefended international boundary without a fence. This bears tribute to the goodwill that exists between the peoples of the United States and Canada.

Waterton-Glacier International Peace Park

Waterton Lakes National Park was established in 1895. Fifteen years later Glacier National Park was formed. In 1932, the same year that Going-to-the-Sun Road was completed, Canada and the United States allied the two parks as the world's first International Peace Park.

The initial driving force for the Peace Park concept came from Rotary Club International. Rotary is a worldwide association of business and professional leaders who offer humanitarian service, encourage high ethical standards in all vocations, and help build goodwill and peace in the world. The main objective of Rotary is service—in the community, in the workplace, and throughout the world. The Rotary Club motto is "Service Above Self." Among the four objectives of the Rotary Club is "The advancement of international understanding, goodwill, and peace through a world fellowship of business and professional persons united in the ideal of service."

In 1931 the Rotary Clubs of Alberta and Montana met to discuss the possibility of the two national parks uniting to form an International Peace Park. The political wheels turned and the two governments were convinced. The next year the Peace Park was established.

Seen first as a gesture to indicate that two nations can solve their problems without military conflict, the concept has evolved to include coordinating resource management concerns.

During 1995, Waterton-Glacier International Peace Park was designated a World Heritage Site by the United Nations. The land that comprises the park has always held sacred meaning to Blackfeet, Kootenai, and Salish peoples. Now it holds special meaning for all the world's citizens.

Kootenai Lakes

The Kootenai Lakes Trail provides a gentle climb to a group of lakes named in honor of Waterton Lakes National Park's first park official, John George "Kootenai" Brown. The immediate vicinity of Kootenai Lakes is prime habitat for moose and black bear.

Level of difficulty: Moderate.

Distance: 5 miles round trip.

Duration: 3–4 hours.

Best time of year: July–September.

Trailhead: The trailhead is left of and behind the Goat Haunt ranger station.

Hiking directions: The first 200 yards of this trail run through an employee housing complex, then the trail splits to the left. At a trail junction another 100 yards beyond you will be directed to go right on the Waterton Valley Trail to Kootenai Falls. For the first 0.3 mile the trail follows an underground water pipeline; it then crosses Cleveland Creek and meanders into the forest.

Special attention: The Kootenai Lakes area is moose habitat. Expect to see them. Stay clear of these large members of the deer family. They can be unpredictable and potentially dangerous.

Notes: The forest is made up primarily of subalpine fir, Douglas fir, and mountain maples. The trail is brushy, with dense forest undergrowth. The dense understory growth includes snowberry, thimbleberry, and myriad wildflowers and grasses. The trail is narrow, winding and flat. As you travel farther into the forest, it becomes dominated by mature Douglas fir trees. The trail heads south through the Waterton Valley with the Waterton River to the west. It passes west of the base of 10,901-foot Mount Cleveland. The trail works its way in and out of an old growth Douglas fir forest and into meadows. In the meadows you will be able to get a look at the Citadel Peaks to the west. The trail enters swampy land after about 2 miles. At 2.2 miles the Kootenai Lakes Trail splits off to the right from the Waterton Valley Trail. The Kootenai Lakes Trail terminates after

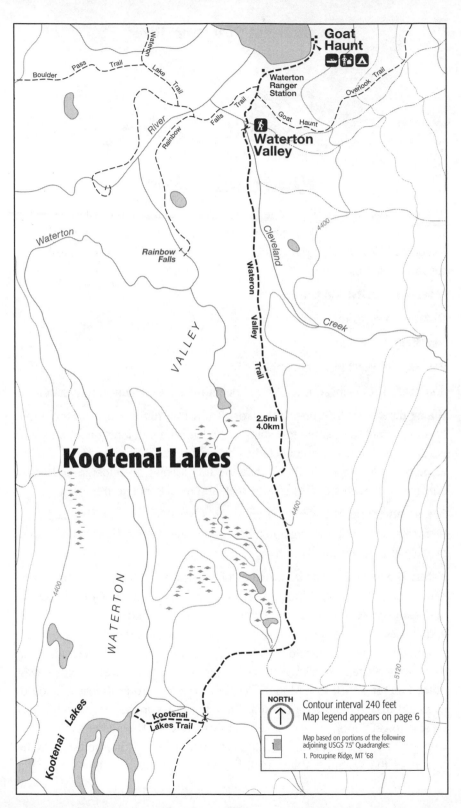

Goat Haunt

Waterton Ranger Station

Waterton Valley

Boulder Pass Trail

Waterton Lake Trail

Overlook Trail

River

Falls Trail

Goat Haunt

Rainbow

Waterton

Rainbow Falls

Cleveland

Creek

4400

VALLEY

Waterton Valley Trail

2.5mi
4.0km

Kootenai Lakes

4400

WATERTON

5120

4400

Kootenai Lakes

Kootenai Lakes Trail

NORTH

Contour interval 240 feet
Map legend appears on page 6

Map based on portions of the following
adjoining USGS 7.5' Quadrangles:

1. Porcupine Ridge, MT '68

0.3 mile in a backcountry campground at the foot of the largest lake in the Kootenai Lakes cluster.

The Kootenai Lakes are a series of small lakes encircled by willows and mountains. The central mountain to the south is 8,542-foot Kootenai Peak.

A bull moose at Kootenai Lakes.

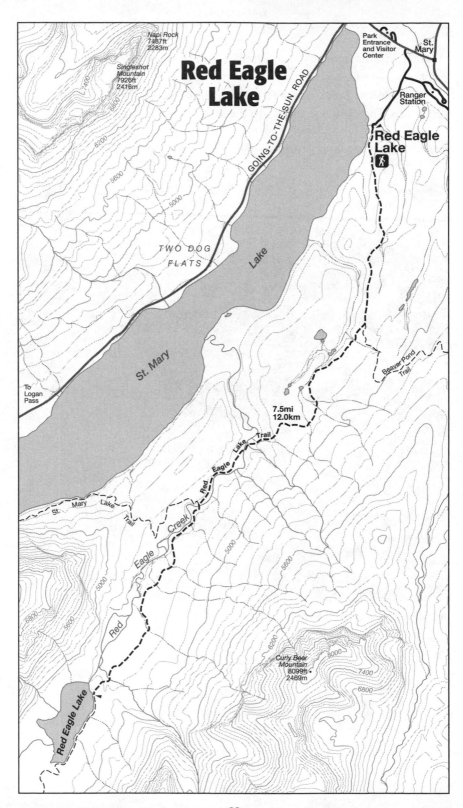

Red Eagle
Lake

Napi Rock
7487ft
2283m

Singleshot
Mountain
7926ft
2416m

GOING-TO-THE-SUN ROAD

Park
Entrance
and Visitor
Center

St.
Mary

Ranger
Station

Red Eagle
Lake

TWO DOG
FLATS

Lake

Beaver Pond
Trail

7.5mi
12.0km

St. Mary

Red Eagle Lake Trail

To
Logan
Pass

St. Mary Lake Trail

Creek

Eagle

Red

Curly Bear
Mountain
8099ft
2469m

Red Eagle Lake

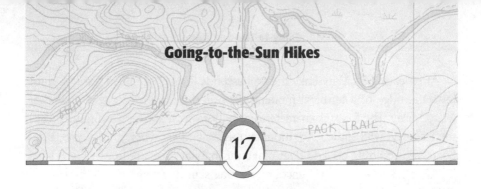

Red Eagle Lake

There are more than 230 species of birds that reside in Glacier National Park during the summer months. The Red Eagle Lake Trail passes through the deciduous forests, parklands, and riparian habitats popular with these species. An early morning departure and late afternoon return will allow birders the chance to enhance their life list.

Level of difficulty: Strenuous.

Distance: 15 miles round trip.

Duration: 7–8 hours.

Best time of year: June–October.

Trailhead: The trail begins at the west end of the large parking lot for the Historic 1913 Ranger Station.

Hiking directions: The trail follows the abandoned Red Eagle roadbed for the first mile. The road follows the shore of St. Mary Lake then moves to the left up a hill. The trail then becomes a narrow hiking path that is well marked and maintained.

Special attention: Begin your hike early to enjoy the beauty of morning sunlight bathing St. Mary Valley and western Red Eagle Valley. Plan on at least 8 hours. This will give you time to investigate the different habitats through which this trail passes.

Notes: Red Eagle Lake is rarely the destination sought by day hikers in Glacier. Most visitors who go to the lake are using it as an overnight camping spot or are continuing past the lake to Triple Divide Pass. Therefore, casual day hikers seldom visit Red Eagle Lake. Because of this, you will not encounter many other visitors on the trail.

Your walk to Red Eagle Lake stretches 7.5 miles through the scenic beauty of a mixed forest, prairie land, and riparian habitats. This walk affords you the opportunity to compare and contrast the flora, the fauna, and the microclimatic characteristics of each environment.

After leaving St. Mary Lake the trail ascends through a mixed forest and follows the ridge of a terminal moraine deposited by the glacier that carved St. Mary Valley. The forest is characterized by flora such as Douglas fir, wild roses, serviceberry, wild strawberry, mountain aster, and snowberry. Gray jays, black bears, red squirrels, elk and deer make this habitat their home.

After 1.3 miles you will encounter a trail sign directing you to the Historic 1913 Ranger Station. This is part of a loop trail known as the Beaver Pond Trail. The Beaver Pond Trail is seldom used. Since it proceeds to the parking lot of the Historic 1913 Ranger Station you may choose to use this as an alternative route back to your car.

At 2 miles you break out into a large meadow. The grand openness is inspirational. From the meadow you will be treated to spectacular panoramic views of Red Eagle Mountain ahead of you, St. Mary Valley and the Logan Pass area to your right, and Flattop Mountain behind you. Near the south side of the meadow you will pass a lone lodgepole pine that has vibrant growth on its lower branches and is dead above. This is typical of a tree that has been partially buried by snow. The snow has protected the lower branches, while the upper branches are exposed to winter winds. Because the ground is frozen and has little available water content the upper branches dry out and die. The effect is known as flagging. Scores of examples of this phenomenon can be seen on Logan Pass.

Listen to the sounds of the quaking aspens along the fringes of the meadow. This habitat is home to prairie grasses and prairie wildflowers, including paintbrush, cinquefoil, pearlyeverlasting, goldenrod, lupine, and coneflower. This and other meadows you will walk through offer an explosion of color in the autumn when the aspen trees and late summer wildflowers are in show.

At about 3 miles you begin to descend into the Red Eagle Creek drainage and its subsequent riparian habitat. You cross the creek by way of a suspension bridge and walk along the lush west bank. This is moose and bear country. Look for their footprints in the mud along the trail. At 4 miles you come to the junction of St. Mary Lake Trail and Red Eagle Lake Trail. At this point you cross back over the creek on a second bridge.

The next 3 miles to Red Eagle Lake are away from the creek and through a moist, mixed, Douglas fir and spruce forest with profuse undergrowth that includes ferns and beargrass.

At 7 miles you cross an intermittent stream, climb a short glacial hill, and break out of the forest to get your first sight of Red Eagle Lake. It is a short distance from the hilltop to the lake. At the lakeshore you can see mountains on three sides. The closest mountain across the lake is 8,881-foot Red Eagle

Mountain. At the end of the lake in the distance is Triple Divide Pass—so named because precipitation falling on a particular point of Triple Divide Peak will enter one of three different river drainages: the Hudson Bay Creek drainage to Hudson Bay, the Atlantic Creek drainage to the Gulf of Mexico, or the Pacific Creek drainage to the Columbia River.

White-tailed deer.

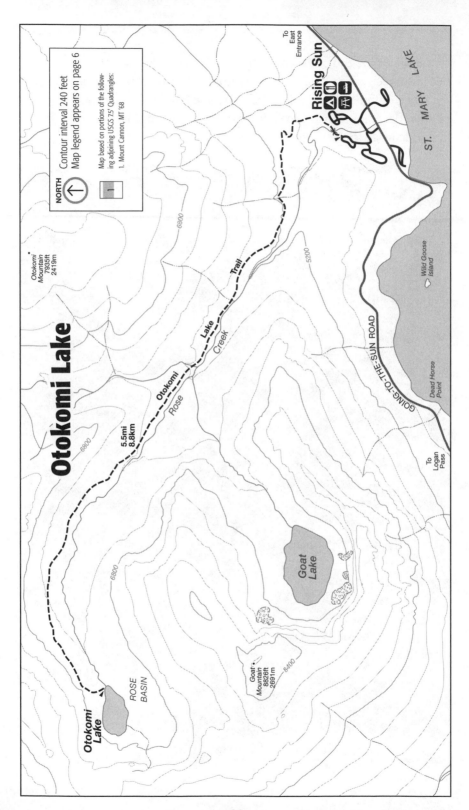

Otokomi Lake

NORTH ⬅

| 1 |

Contour interval 240 feet
Map legend appears on page 6

Map based on portions of the following adjoining USGS 7.5' Quadrangles:
1. Mount Cannon, MT '68

Otokomi
Mountain
7935ft
2419m

6800

6800

6800

Otokomi Lake Trail

Rose Creek

5.5mi
8.8km

ROSE BASIN

Otokomi
Lake

Goat
Mountain
8826ft
2691m

6400

Goat
Lake

Rising Sun

⬅ 🏕 🏚 🛒 🏚

To East
Entrance

5200

GOING-TO-THE-SUN ROAD

Dead Horse
Point

To Logan
Pass

Wild Goose
Island

ST. MARY LAKE

Otokomi Lake

Otokomi means "Yellow Fish" in the Blackfeet language. The lake is named after a Blackfeet guide. This tarn sits in an alpine basin, fed all summer long by melting snow.

Level of difficulty: Strenuous.

Distance: 11 miles round trip.

Duration: 5–6 hours.

Best time of year: July–October.

Trailhead: The trailhead to Otokomi Lake is to the left of the camp store at Rising Sun. There is ample parking available near the trailhead.

Hiking directions: The trail has only one destination, Otokomi Lake. The trail is well marked and easy to follow.

Special attention: Dense forest undergrowth along the trail will retain water after rain or morning dew. Wear water-resistant clothing.

Notes: The walk to Otokomi Lake affords you the chance to experience a stream drainage from St. Mary Lake to the headwaters at Otokomi Lake. The drainage, Rose Creek, is dominated by a series of cascades, waterfalls, pools and fast-moving water. The Otokomi Lake Trail takes you into a drainage that can only be glimpsed from Going-to-the-Sun Road. From the road, one can only imagine what lies in the valley. One of the reasons to make this hike is to see the outstanding colorful rocks that make up the Rose Basin in which Otokomi Lake sits. The reds, greens, and yellows are striking in contrast and beauty, particularly when viewed on a clear day.

The trail follows the east side of Rose Creek. The flora of the area is typical of the lower St. Mary Valley. It consists of juniper, Douglas fir, black cottonwood, maple, buffaloberry, chokecherry, wild rose, serviceberry, Oregon grape, thimbleberry, mountain aster, fireweed, harebell, Indian paintbrush, and beargrass. Meriwether Lewis named beargrass, a member of the lily family, believing that it serves as food for bears. Naturalists have since learned that bears do not usually eat it.

Leaving the creek you follow a one-lane path with soft footing. The trail winds uphill in a series of easy switchbacks. The first mile is in deep forest of mostly Douglas fir and lodgepole pine, with a few western larches.

When the trail breaks out high above Rose Creek you will have a commanding view of 8,826-foot Goat Mountain in front of you. The trail then follows high above swirling Rose Creek. The occasional glimpses you receive of rushing Rose Creek are impressive. When you once again meet up with Rose Creek you will be in a large avalanche chute. Note the jumble of trees on your side of the creek and observe the size of the avalanche chute. Imagine the magnitude of the event that took place here several years ago, and the reaction of the Park Service trail-clearing crew when they saw the trees spread like pick-up sticks.

After passing the avalanche chute you begin a series of short, gentle switchbacks through a forest of western white pine and huckleberry bushes. Look for Stellar jays, gray jays, chipmunks, and golden-mantled ground squirrels.

As you approach the lake you will cross a large talus slope and avalanche area. It is easy to look at the surrounding topography and visualize the glacial action that carved the U-shaped valley. Otokomi Lake is a cirque lake sitting in Rose Basin; lofty, snow-covered, red argillite peaks rise high above the timberline. Talus slopes from Goat Mountain come down to the lake from the southwest. The view of the basin is a panorama of sheer beauty.

Baring Falls

The walk to Baring Falls gives you an introduction to the St. Mary Lake area.

Level of difficulty: Easy.

Distance: 1.4 miles round trip.

Duration: 1 hour.

Best time of year: June–October.

Trailhead: The trailhead is located at the southeast corner of the large Sun Point parking lot off Going-to-the-Sun Road.

Hiking directions: The trail to Baring Falls follows the Sun Point Nature Trail and is a gentle pathway along the north shore of St. Mary Lake.

Special attention: The Glacier Natural History Association and the National Park Service have provided a Sun Point Nature Trail Guide. You can acquire the guide for 50 cents at the trailhead. The guide identifies stops along the trail and is a good introduction to the natural and cultural history of the St. Mary Lake area.

Notes: The rocky, heavily used, and well-maintained trail immediately descends toward St. Mary Lake. It soon splits with the main trail going to the right and a spur trail to the left. Follow the left-hand spur trail to Sun Point. At the Point you will find an informational direction finder that shows the mountains in the immediate area. Sun Point provides a good panoramic view of Citadel, Little Chief, and Going-to-the-Sun Mountains to the west and Red Eagle Mountain, Curly Bear Mountain, and Single Shot Mountain to the east. You also get a good view of St. Mary Lake. At 9.6 miles long, 0.25 mile wide, and 289 feet deep, St. Mary Lake is the second largest lake in Glacier National Park. With a little imagination you can visualize how 10,000 years ago glaciers "bulldozed" the St. Mary area leaving the hanging valleys and the large lake as testament to their awesome earth-shaping power.

Return to the trail junction and follow the main trail to the west. You will soon come to the site where the Great Northern Railroad built the Going-to-the-Sun Chalets in 1913. The chalet complex consisted of nine buildings perched 100 feet above St. Mary Lake. The buildings included a main lodge for dining, an employee dorm, and guest sleeping quarters. Inattention to mainte-

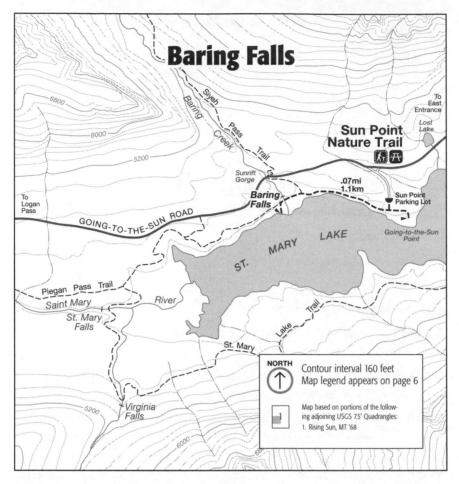

Baring Falls

Slyeh
Baring Creek
Pass Trail

To
East
Entrance

Lost
Lake

**Sun Point
Nature Trail**

Sunrift
Gorge

To
Logan
Pass

.07mi
1.1km

**Baring
Falls**

Sun Point
Parking Lot

GOING-TO-THE-SUN ROAD

ST. MARY LAKE

Going-to-the-Sun
Point

Piegan Pass Trail

Saint Mary

St. Mary
Falls

River

Lake Trail

St. Mary

NORTH

Contour interval 160 feet
Map legend appears on page 6

Map based on portions of the following adjoining USGS 7.5' Quadrangles:
1. Rising Sun, MT '68

Virginia
Falls

nance funds caused the chalets to fall into disrepair. Visitors no longer came. The chalets became unprofitable and were razed by burning in 1949.

The trail traverses the northern shore of the lake along a rocky pathway, sometimes through forest and sometimes out in the open. The trees of the forest are mostly Douglas fir, subalpine fir, western white pine, lodgepole pine, and aspen. Although there is a healthy understory of plants, this area is not noted for its wildflower display. Instead, it provides some wonderful vistas of St. Mary Lake and its valley.

You will soon see a footbridge that crosses Baring Creek. To the right of the footbridge is Baring Falls, at one time named Water Ouzal (dipper) Falls for its resident dippers. Look for dippers flying, wading, and bobbing near the waterfall. The waters these dippers call home comes from Sexton Glacier, high on 9,642-foot Going-to-the-Sun Mountain.

A short walk down the trail beyond Baring Creek will take you to St. Mary Lake and a boat dock used by the Glacier Park Company for their boat trips.

St. Mary Falls and Virginia Falls

Be sure to bring your camera on this short hike. The combination of wildflowers in the meadows, the cascading streams, and the beautiful waterfalls makes this an exceptionally photogenic area.

Level of difficulty: Easy.

Distance: St. Mary Falls 2.4 miles round trip; Virginia Falls 3.6 miles round trip.

Duration: 2–3 hours.

Best time of year: June–October.

Trailhead: The St. Mary Falls pullout, 10.5 miles west of St. Mary on Going-to-the-Sun Road, is the trailhead. There is enough parking for sixteen cars. During July–August plan to arrive early in the morning or late in the afternoon to increase your chances of finding a parking spot.

Hiking directions: Follow St. Mary Falls Trail. The trail is well marked.

Notes: The St. Mary Falls Trail receives heavy use, is well maintained, and is easy to walk. The forest is made up mostly of Douglas fir and maple trees. The understory plant growth consists of beargrass, snowberry, and thimbleberry bushes.

Within 200 feet of the trailhead you will come to a small south-facing meadow. This meadow displays a profusion of wildflowers throughout the growing season. Trees to the north of the meadow frame Going-to-the-Sun Mountain as it looms overhead at 9,642 feet. Little Chief Mountain, elevation 9,541 feet, emerges to the south.

The trail at this point is laid out over red argillite rock. Look for ripple marks in the large slab pieces along the side of the trail. These ripple marks are the result of wave action in water on mud millions of years ago. The water receded and the mud hardened, eventually turning to stone. The hard mud was buried under subsequent layers of sedimentary rock but later exposed as a result of erosion and mountain building. The mudstone contains an appreciable amount of oxidized iron, giving it its red color.

The St. Mary River is made up of water draining from the Siyeh Pass and

St. Mary Falls and Virginia Falls

Piegan Pass areas to the north, and the Blackfoot Glacier and Jackson Glacier to the south. It also carries the water from the Hanging Gardens on the east side of Logan Pass.

A footbridge passes over the St. Mary River just below St. Mary Falls. You should see at least one dipper near the base of the waterfall. Dippers live along this fast-moving river, making their moss nests close to the water line. The footbridge is near the confluence of St. Mary River and Virginia Creek. Great volumes of water intermingle here, most notably in June and early July when the alpine snowfields melt. At this time of the season you can expect this area to enrapture you with its beautiful sights and thundering sounds while you feel the chilly swirling spray of St. Mary Falls, a delightful respite on a hot July day.

The trail extends to Virginia Falls along Virginia Creek. The creek is a series of cataracts, pools, and swift-moving water. Soon after encountering the creek the trail proceeds up a series of rocklike steps and over a small wooden bridge to a large cataract. You will hear Virginia Falls long before you see it. A footbridge crosses Virginia Creek below the waterfall. The water that makes up Virginia Creek mostly comes from the Citadel Mountain and Almost-a-Dog Mountain areas to the south. No major glacier adds water to Virginia Creek.

Hidden Lake

An estimated 2,500 to 3,500 people visit Logan Pass on any given day in July and August. A large percentage of these visitors will walk at least part of the Hidden Lake Trail. The 1.5-mile walk to the Hidden Lake Overlook is the most popular hike in Glacier National Park. This overlook is half the distance to Hidden Lake. The remaining distance to the lake is highlighted with outstanding alpine scenery.

Level of difficulty: Easy.

Distance: 6 miles round trip.

Duration: 3–4 hours.

Best time of year: July–October.

Trailhead: Hidden Lake Trailhead is directly behind the Logan Pass Visitor Center. There is limited parking available. The lot may fill by 10:00 A.M. and remain full until 4:00 P.M. during the height of summer. You may avoid parking difficulties by using the hiker shuttle service. Check with the concessionaire for times and cost.

Hiking directions: The first 0.25 mile of the trail to Hidden Lake is paved. It then becomes a boardwalk for the next 0.25 mile. The remainder of the trail to the Hidden Lake Overlook is well established and wide. The trail is a single-lane dirt path from the overlook to Hidden Lake. The Glacier Natural History Association in cooperation with the National Park Service provides a trail guide for the walk to the overlook. You can purchase the guide for 50 cents at the trailhead.

Special attention: Expect to find many visitors along the 1.5-mile walk to the overlook. Most visitors do not explore beyond this point, maybe because the 500 feet elevation change is challenge enough. This is regrettable because the best views of Hidden Lake and the immediate mountains are only a few hundred feet beyond the overlook.

Notes: Be sure to spend time looking at the exhibits in the Logan Pass Visitor Center. The exhibits are well designed and effectively interpret the natural history of the area.

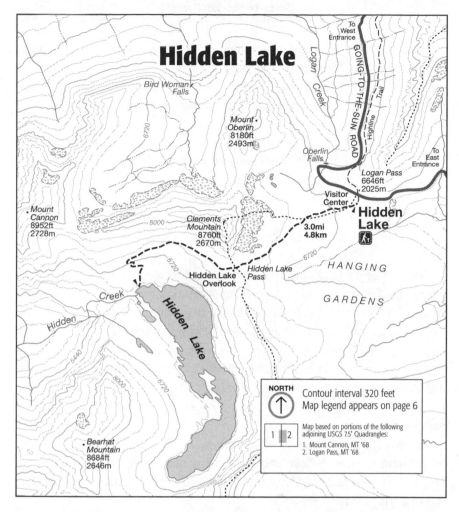

Embarking on the trail you will walk through a changing panorama of alpine meadow views interspersed with small pockets of storm-gnarled subalpine fir trees. The thrust-up snow-capped peaks that dominate the skyline are from left to right, Reynolds Mountain at 9,125 feet, Clements Mountain at 8,760 feet, and Mount Oberlin at 8,180 feet. Mount Oberlin is the prominent landmark in front of you. Water flows from its slopes, composing a medley of sounds. The trail passes over several of these rivulets. They provide excellent photographic opportunities of the rushing water, wildflowers, and mountain backdrops.

You may also be able to photograph the myriad wildflowers that bloom during the short growing season. There are approximately 1,000 species of vascular plants that grow in Glacier. During July and August (the height of the flowering season) it seems that all of the species live along the Hidden Lake Trail. The outburst of color, and the diversity of the blooming plants in this alpine area is stunning. Among the most showy flowers are the glacier lily, mountain aster, monkeyflower, and beargrass. The plants have only a few days to bloom, be pollinated, and begin seed development. Some plants, like the glacier lily, begin growing under the snow. They push up through the snow and flower as the snow is melting.

Along the trail you will encounter several denizens of Logan Pass: golden-mantled ground squirrels, Columbian ground squirrels, pikas, hoary marmots, and the monarchs of the high ranges, mountain goats. Like the flowering plants on which most of them feed, they have a short season in which to complete the cycle of life. Don't be surprised if they seem indifferent to your presence. They have only a few weeks to mate and store fat so they can survive the long winter.

Look for ripple marks on some of the red rocks along the trail. These rocks are red argillite. Millions of years ago they were mud with a high concentration of iron. The ripple marks are the result of water action in the shallows of a sea. The sea evaporated, the mud dried, and the iron in the mud oxidized into the characteristic red color. After millions of years of compression from above, these ripple marks became part of sedimentary rock. The rocks were uplifted during a prolonged mountain building episode about 50 million years ago. Subsequent erosion of the layers of rock above the ripple-marked rocks have left them exposed for you to enjoy.

You will reach the Hidden Lake Overlook at 1.5 miles. Stand on the wooden platform to view the lake and surrounding mountains. On a calm day the lake will be mirror-clear and seem to be in a reflective mood. On windy days the lake will glimmer with color.

The trail proceeds to the west along the slope of Mount Oberlin. Look for remnants of a once-buried telephone line exposed along the trail as you descend to Hidden Lake. This line, laid by the Civilian Conservation Corps in 1938, connected the Logan Pass area to stations at Hidden Lake and at Avalanche Lake.

Soon the eastern end of Lake McDonald comes into view, and you will see Hidden Lake. Hidden Lake, named Bear Hat Lake by the Kootenai, with its many islets, appears to wrap around the base of 8,684-foot Bear Hat Mountain. The walk from the overlook to Hidden Lake is an 800-foot descent. It is deemed moderate in difficulty. Yield to uphill hikers as you are descending to the lake. You will appreciate the courtesy upon your return.

Columbian Ground Squirrels

These rather large colonial ground squirrels range throughout Glacier National Park. Their high-pitched chirp can be heard from most trails, and colonies of Columbian ground squirrels can be seen around the Logan Pass Visitor Center. If these squirrels seem indifferent to your presence it is because they are accustomed to humans and see you as no threat. Also, they are too busy feeding in order to store fat for the long winter to pay attention to you. These squirrels hibernate up to seven months. They enter hibernation when their green vegetative food supply begins to dry up. Depending on local conditions, this could happen in late July. Certainly by mid-August all of Glacier's Columbian ground squirrels have gone into hibernation. As they hibernate their pulse falls as low as 35 beats per minute. The males emerge from hibernation at least two weeks before the females, usually in March, but it could be later depending on snow depths.

Local people often refer to Columbian grownd squirrels as gophers. They belong to a family of animals that includes marmots, prairie dogs, chipmunks, flying squirrels, and tree quirrels; gophers belong to a different family that is made up of gophers alone. The only gopher in Glacier National Park is the 6-inch-long Northern pocket gopher.

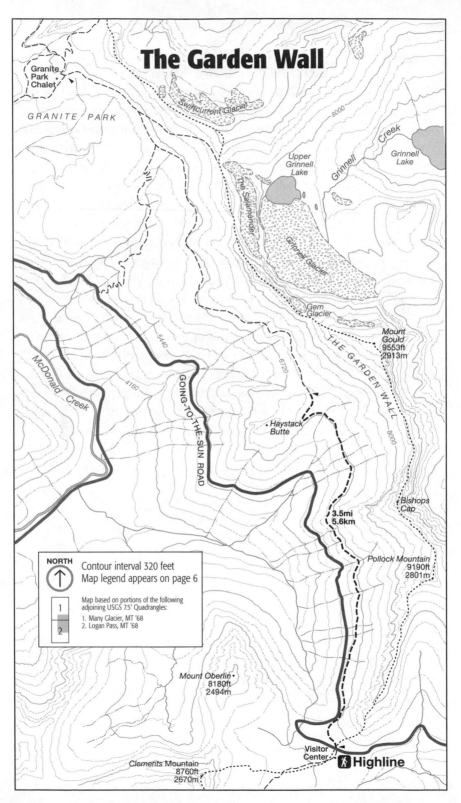

The Garden Wall

Granite Park Chalet

GRANITE PARK

Swiftcurrent Glacier

8000

Grinnell Creek

Upper Grinnell Lake

The Salamander

Grinnell Lake

Grinnell Glacier

Gem Glacier

McDonald Creek

5440

6720

THE GARDEN WALL

Mount Gould
9553ft
2913m

4160

GOING-TO-THE-SUN ROAD

Haystack Butte

8000

3.5mi
5.6km

Bishops Cap

Pollock Mountain
9190ft
2801m

NORTH
↑

Contour interval 320 feet
Map legend appears on page 6

1
2

Map based on portions of the following adjoining USGS 7.5' Quadrangles:

1. Many Glacier, MT '68
2. Logan Pass, MT '68

Mount Oberlin
8180ft
2494m

Visitor Center

Clements Mountain
8760ft
2670m

🚶 Highline

22

The Garden Wall

The Garden Wall provides a unique hiking experience. Situated high above and in sight of Going-to-the-Sun Road, the trail takes you through flower gardens and tumbling cascades that many backyard gardeners would like to imitate.

Level of difficulty: Easy.

Distance: 7 miles round trip.

Duration: 4–5 hours.

Best time of year: July–October.

Trailhead: The trailhead is across Going-to-the-Sun Road from the Logan Pass Visitor Center. There is limited parking available. The lot may fill by 10:00 A.M. and remain full until 4:00 P.M. You may want to avoid parking difficulties by using the hiker shuttle service. Check with the concessionaire for times and cost.

Hiking directions: Take the well marked and frequented Highline Trail.

Special attention: One of the reasons there are profuse wildflower displays along the Garden Wall is abundant surface water. Be prepared for a great deal of water flowing across the trail.

Notes: Many visitors explore only the first 0.25 mile of this trail. Some people will turn back when they realize that to continue on the trail they must walk along a narrow ledge high above Going-to-the-Sun Road.

It is in this first 0.25 mile that you will likely see mountain goats. They live on steep slopes and benches along cliffs. Mountain goats have pointed hooves and soft foot-pads that allow them to hop along precipitous outcroppings. They feed on vegetation, usually above timberline.

Begin your walk in the early morning in order to take advantage of the soft sunlight bathing Reynolds Mountain, Heaven's Peak, the Livingston Range, and your destination, Haystack Butte.

In addition to the abundant flowers, you will come upon plentiful wildlife, regardless of the summer month during which you choose to hike this trail. It is common to spot ptarmigans, mountain goats, hoary marmots, pikas, chip-

Mountain goat along Highline Trail.

munks, golden-mantled ground squirrels, Columbian ground squirrels, and even bears along this track. The best time of year to enjoy the most wildflowers and wildlife is August, although the wildflowers will last well into September.

At the Haystack Butte saddle you will be between Haystack Mountain on the west and Mount Gould on the right. The mountain in front of you and to the right is Mount Grinnell.

At this 7,000-foot elevation, snow will last past Labor Day. Here you can witness "springtime" arriving in September. At the Haystack saddle you will be able to see wildflowers beginning to come forth as the snow melts. Observe the area radiating away from the snowfield and notice the plants successively maturing as they break through the soil to the state of flowering. The growing season is very short in this alpine zone. Few annual plant species live here. They do not have time to germinate from seed, grow, bloom, be polinated, and set seeds before killings frosts. Consequently, most of the plants are perennials, living more than 2 years. Because the plants are mature after the second year they can use the entire growing season for reproduction and food storage. By October they will need to bud, bloom, pollinate, have time for seeds to mature, and grow enough to store energy in their roots for the next nine to ten months. Some of the perennial plants you enjoy along this trail may be many years older than you—many species can have individual plants over 100 years old.

We often think of these alpine areas as harsh environments for the plants. Keep in mind that these flora are well adapted to this life zone. The climate of your backyard would be "harsh" to these plants.

Johns Lake Loop

During the hot summer months you will likely find this walk through a forest of western red cedar, mountain hemlock, and western larch a cool and refreshing respite.

Level of difficulty: Easy.

Distance: 3 miles round trip.

Duration: 1–2 hours.

Best time of year: June–October.

Trailhead: The trailhead is 1.5 miles east of Lake McDonald Lodge on the south side of Going-to-the-Sun Road. There is adequate parking for up to eight cars. The sign at the trailhead reads "Johns Lake, 0.5 mile."

Special attention: This loop trail parallels McDonald Creek next to McDonald Falls. There are dangerous dropoff areas along this portion of the trail. Small children should be closely monitored.

Hiking directions: Follow the trail to Johns Lake. You may choose to unite the McDonald Creek Trail with the Johns Lake Trail in order to make a loop back to your car. Completing the loop will take you along McDonald Creek, past McDonald Falls, and near the head of Lake McDonald. The entire trip is about 3 miles.

Notes: The trail is smooth with good footing. It is very wide in the beginning due to the fact that hikers accessing other destinations and horseback riders from the park's concessionaire use it.

The walk to Johns Lake is a favorite short hike enjoyed by families with young children. The trail offers many visual delights. Lots of fungi and flowers grow on the forest floor. This is home to deer and black bears. Children enjoy listening for the chattering of red squirrels. This is also habitat for nocturnal flying squirrels and the predators of both species of squirrels: owls and martens.

Immediately after leaving the parking lot you step into the magical forest of young mountain hemlocks and western red cedar trees. Scattered among the

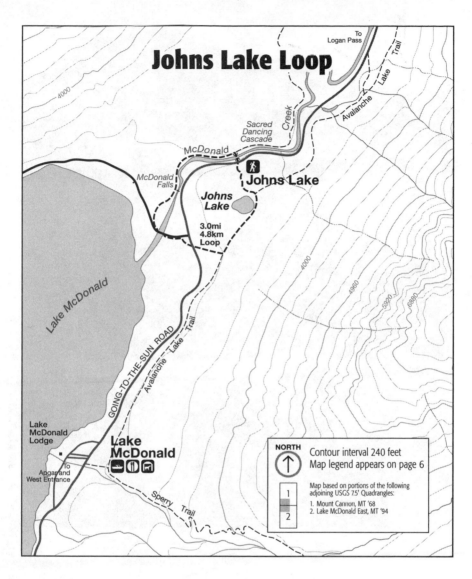

Johns Lake Loop

To Logan Pass

Avalanche Lake Trail

Creek

Sacred Dancing Cascade

McDonald

Johns Lake

McDonald Falls

Johns Lake

3.0mi
4.8km
Loop

Lake McDonald

GOING-TO-THE-SUN ROAD

Avalanche Lake Trail

Lake McDonald Lodge

Lake McDonald

To Apgar and West Entrance

Sperry Trail

NORTH

Contour interval 240 feet
Map legend appears on page 6

Map based on portions of the following adjoining USGS 7.5' Quadrangles:

1. Mount Cannon, MT '68
2. Lake McDonald East, MT '94

conifers are mountain maple trees that glow with red and yellow leaves in the autumn. The forest understory includes huckleberry and snowberry bushes that add their own distinctive colors in the fall and lovely fruit in the summer. The forest floor is carpeted with thick layers of mosses and numerous varieties of fungi. Look for tooth marks on the caps of mushrooms. Voles, mice, and squirrels will include mushrooms as part of their diet, eating just a bit and leaving the rest. Sometimes you see a mushroom cap lodged in the branches of a conifer. A resident red squirrel has cached it for a future meal.

It is a relatively short walk to Johns Lake. The lake is small and shallow and completely surrounded by forest. The edge of the lake is lined with water lily plants. The two mountains to the north that serve as the backdrop to Johns

Johns Lake.

Lake are Stanton Mountain at 7,750 feet in elevation and 8,850-foot Mount Vaught. You will see them again when you reach Going-to-the-Sun Road.

Continue on the trail to the head of the lake. At this point you will encounter a sign directing the way to Avalanche Lake. Stay on the Johns Lake Trail to the left. The trail is laid out away from the lake and into a mature fairyland-like forest. High above the forest floor is a canopy of mountain hemlock. Little direct sunlight penetrates the dense forest overstory. This results in an open forest floor with a luxuriant velvety green carpet of moss. Notice that the boulders are draped in the soft, thick plant life. Even with overcast skies, everything in the forest glows because of soft light reflecting off the verdant mosses.

The forest is composed almost completely of mature mountain hemlock trees. The few smaller trees are hemlock, as well. This is a climax forest. No new tree species will replace the hemlocks. Succession has come to an end. The next event in the process will be a forest fire or "blow-down" of the trees. This event will allow light to reach the forest floor and a new forest will begin. Pioneer trees species such as alder, lodgepole pine, and/or western larch will take hold. It may take hundreds of years of forest succession before the mountain hemlock is the dominate tree once more.

You will soon hear the rushing waters of McDonald Creek and sounds from cars on Going-to-the-Sun Road. The trail will lead you to a walkway that crosses the road and to a paved footpath to McDonald Creek. A wooden bridge spans the creek. Proceed on the trail to the left after crossing the creek.

You will now share the trail with horseback riders until you come to a small sign with a picture of a person riding a horse with a red line drawn through it. At this juncture the trail splits. You need to walk to the left of the sign and follow the inconspicuous trail along the creek. The trail soon becomes evident.

Look for harlequin ducks in the waters of McDonald Creek. The harlequin is a small duck native to North America, Iceland, and eastern Siberia. This delightfully beautiful small duck has blue and red plumage with black and white markings that give the male a clownlike appearance, hence its common name. Harlequins are generally silent birds, so you will need to look for them closely. They appear along McDonald Creek in late June, looking for nesting spots. By mid-August the harlequins have left Glacier and have returned to their winter habitat along the rocky coastline of the Pacific Northwest.

The trail passes cascades formed by water passing over dozens of tilted layered limestone rocks. The effect of the cascade is enhanced as the water level in the creek drops late in the summer season. At that time of year the creek is a progression of eddies and multihued small pools, as the water reflects the colors of the forest and the sky.

After the cascade the trail approaches McDonald Falls. After the falls the trail winds back into the cedar/hemlock forest. You will soon come to a paved spur road that goes to a ranger station and trailheads to Trout Lake and the north shore of Lake McDonald. Turn to the left and follow the road over the bridge of McDonald Creek. The view from the bridge provides an excellent vantage point for photographing Lake McDonald and the distant Apgar Mountains. Early morning and sunset times are best for capturing this remarkable viewpoint with a camera, or within your own memory.

After crossing the bridge look for the trail on the right side of the road. You will want to follow this trail back to your car. The trail keeps you from walking along the shoulder of the Going-to-the-Sun Road.

Trail of the Cedars.

(24)

Trail of the Cedars

This is perhaps the most popular loop trail in Glacier National Park, and for good reason. The loop is short, easy, and has beautifully diverse scenery.

Level of difficulty: Easy.

Distance: 0.7 mile round trip.

Duration: 1 hour.

Best time of year: June–September.

Trailhead: The trailhead is immediately east of Avalanche Creek Campground along Going-to-the-Sun Road.

Hiking directions: Begin your hike on the boardwalk. This means that you will complete your hike on a paved surface.

Special attention: This is a very popular area within the park. Visitors are spending time at McDonald Creek, hiking to Avalanche Lake, and walking the Trail of the Cedars. Parking is limited in this congested area. Plan to arrive before 10:00 A.M. or after 5:00 P.M. during the height of the visitor season in order to increase your chances of finding a parking spot.

Notes: The National Park Service and the Glacier Natural History Association have installed signs along the boardwalk to interpret the natural history of this outstanding ecosystem. The interpretive signs invite you to become in-tune with your surroundings. This is a wonderful trail to walk slowly, to stop and linger, to smell the fragrances, to notice lighting differences, and to feel the temperature variations of an ancient forest.

The hike leads you through a grove of old growth western red cedar and black cottonwood. Some of the western red cedar trees are more than 350 years old. The smaller trees in the forest are mountain hemlocks. Notice their characteristic drooped tops. The tall and dense canopy of the cedar trees allows little direct light to penetrate to the forest floor. Mountain hemlock is shade tolerant and can grow under these conditions. The remaining understory is sparse

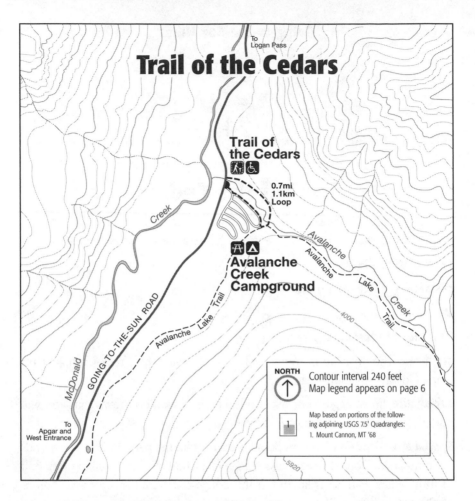

Trail of the Cedars

To Logan Pass

Trail of the Cedars

0.7mi
1.1km
Loop

Creek

Avalanche

Avalanche

Avalanche Lake

Creek Trail

Avalanche Creek Campground

Avalanche Lake Trail

GOING-TO-THE-SUN ROAD

McDonald

4000

To Apgar and West Entrance

5920

NORTH
Contour interval 240 feet
Map legend appears on page 6

Map based on portions of the following adjoining USGS 7.5' Quadrangles:
1. Mount Cannon, MT '68

because of the low light conditions. The forest floor is carpeted with ferns, mosses, and a wide array of fungi.

The first half of the trail is on a boardwalk. The trail turns into a footpath after crossing a bridge over Avalanche Creek. Avalanche Creek near the footbridge is one of the most photographed locations in the park. The rushing creek exits a narrow canyon composed of red argillite rock. The effect is striking and photo-scenic.

Immediately after the bridge the trail to Avalanche Lake strikes off to the south. It climbs briefly before leveling along the Avalanche Creek Canyon. This is also a good place for photographs because the swirling waters, turquoise pools, and sculpted red argillite have dramatic interplay effects. This short side trip from the Trail of the Cedars will give you a chance to see dippers along the creek and take note of the myriad sounds that the hastening waters compose.

The remaining Trail of the Cedars is a paved footpath. There are several places along the way to sit near the creek to enjoy the splendor of the area. This section of the trail is in an abandoned loop of the Avalanche Creek Campground. The campground was one of the facilities improved by the Civilian Conservation Corps (CCC) in the early 1930s. It was closed several years ago to allow the area to re-vegetate. There are no plans to re-open the loop, in favor of leaving it part of the Trail of the Cedars Loop.

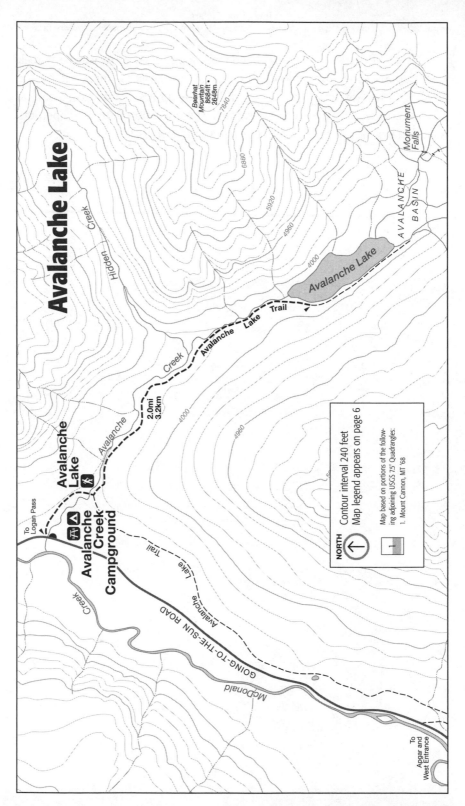

Avalanche Lake

Bearhat
Mountain
8684ft •
2648m

7840

6880

5920

4960

4000

Monument
Falls

AVALANCHE BASIN

Avalanche Lake

Avalanche Lake Trail

Creek

Hidden

Creek

4000

2.0mi
3.2km

Avalanche

4000

4960

4960

Avalanche
Lake

Avalanche
Creek
Campground

To
Logan Pass

Avalanche Lake Trail

GOING-TO-THE-SUN ROAD

McDonald Creek

To
Apgar and
West Entrance

NORTH

Contour interval 240 feet
Map legend appears on page 6

Map based on portions of the following adjoining USGS 7.5' Quadrangles:
1. Mount Cannon, MT '68

1

Avalanche Lake

Avalanche Lake is one of the most popular destinations in Glacier National Park. This short walk will make it obvious why so many cars are in the trailhead parking lot.

Level of difficulty: Easy.

Distance: 4 miles round trip.

Duration: 2–3 hours.

Best time of year: June–October.

Trailhead: The Avalanche Lake Trailhead is at the far end of the Trail of the Cedars. The trail is well marked and obvious.

Hiking directions: Almost all hikers using this trail will have Avalanche Lake as their destination.

Special attention: This trail receives heavy use by hikers. Even so, bears frequent the area. Early morning and late evening solo hiking can put you at additional risk. Be alert and use the National Park Service guidelines you received at the entrance station to help avoid a confrontation.

Notes: The first 0.3 mile of the trail is worthy of exploration even if you do not have Avalanche Lake as your hiking goal. The lower segment of the trail passes through the Avalanche Creek Canyon. Here, over thousands of years, the whirling waters have shaped and polished the red argillite rock into a beautifully sculpted watercourse. As you stand admiring the churning waters in the gorge you might be startled by a bird zipping through your field of view. This small gray bird is a water ouzel, also known as a dipper. Dippers live near fast-moving water. They stay in Glacier year round.

Just beyond the trailhead the Avalanche Lake Trail climbs 500 feet through a forest of western hemlock, western red cedar, western larch, mountain maple, spruce, and black cottonwood. The open forest floor, and red argillite rock that has been sculpted by the creek, makes up the trailbed. The forest floor has a heavy matting of verdant mosses.

Notice the many trees that have fallen in the forest, several across the trail.

Avalanche Creek.

National Park Service trail crews clear these trees from the trail so that you can have easy access to Avalanche Lake. In the spring it is necessary to use gas-powered chainsaws due to the volume of work. When the trail crews have cleared most of the primary trails, they revert to handsaws. The use of handsaws mitigates noise pollution and keeps alive the traditions of the past, while providing an opportunity for trail crew personnel to interact with visitors and teach them historic logging practices and woodsmanship.

Above the canyon and along the trail the trees in the forest are recognizably shorter, smaller in diameter, and more closely spaced.

As you get near the lake, the forest floor changes. More sunlight reaches the floor and this encourages the growth of bracken ferns. Other understory plants in the forest include thimbleberry and elderberry.

At an elevation of 3,905 feet, Avalanche Lake, originally called Beaver Head Lake by the Kootenai, sits in a narrow valley that was once glaciated. As the glacier melted, it left a depression that filled with run-off. Today much of the water comes from the area of Sperry Glacier. As you face the lake the mountains from left to right are Bear Hat Mountain (8,684 feet), Fusillade Mountain (8,750 feet), Little Matterhorn (7,886 feet), and Mount Brown (8,565 feet). Depending on the time of year, you may see as many as five large cascades feeding the lake. The waterfall between Bearhat Mountain and Fusillade Mountain is Monument Falls. Sperry Glacier is in a hanging cirque valley between Fusillade Mountain and Little Matterhorn. Sperry Glacier cannot be seen from the lake.

Dippers

Look for bird droppings on the boulders in the creek. These droppings provide evidence that dippers or water ouzels (the British name) are living in the area. If you do not see the droppings listen for the sharp "zeet" call. Dippers are slate-gray, six-inch-long birds. They are about the size of an immature robin, but with a short tail. The dipper's habitat ranges from Alaska to Central America, from the eastern Rocky Mountain Front to the Pacific Coast. They are common along the fast-moving streams in Glacier National Park. Dippers get their common name from their characteristic bobbing mannerisms. Dippers are solitary birds that build their nests out of mosses near fast-moving water, often next to or behind waterfalls. They have special oil glands that allow their feathers to stay dry. Their strong yellowish legs allow them to walk underwater in order to catch insects. They have been known to flap their wings and "fly" underwater. Dippers are fun to watch as they walk into swiftly moving water and disappear. You can only guess where they will emerge.

Fish Lake

Fish Lake is an endearing small lake set within a dense forest. This is one of the few lakes in Glacier National Park in which towering mountains do not dominate the skyline.

Level of difficulty: Easy.

Distance: 6 miles round trip.

Duration: 2–3 hours.

Best time of year: June–September.

Trailhead: The trail to Fish Lake begins at the Sperry Trailhead on the south side of Going-to-the-Sun Road across from the Lake McDonald Lodge parking lot.

Hiking directions: The trail is well marked. Beyond the Sperry Trailhead is a sign designating the trail as the Gunsight Pass Trail. Follow the Gunsight Pass Trail for 2 miles. The Snyder Ridge Fire Trail splits to the right after you cross Snyder Creek, the first major creek you encounter.

Notes: The trail ascends 1,000 feet through a forest of western red cedar, western larch, western hemlock, mountain maple, and spruce. The first part of the trail is heavily used as it funnels access to Sperry Chalet, Sperry Glacier, Mount Brown Lookout, Snyder Lake, and Gunsight Pass, as well as Fish Lake. Within the first 0.25 mile you will pass a horse barn and an abandoned sewage treatment facility. The lower reaches of the trail are used by the horse concession of Glacier Park.

Continue straight when you come to a sign that identifies the trail as Gunsight Pass Trail and points out the direction to Sperry Chalet. The creek that you hear to your right is Snyder Creek. This area of the forest is dominated by mature western hemlock and western red cedar. The undergrowth includes bearberry, twinflower, beargrass, pearlyeverlasting, numerous species of mosses, and many different fungi. The trail is smooth and moderate in its ascent through the forest. After 0.3 mile the trail passes an overlook with views of Snyder Creek and the head of Lake McDonald. Howe Ridge is the dominant

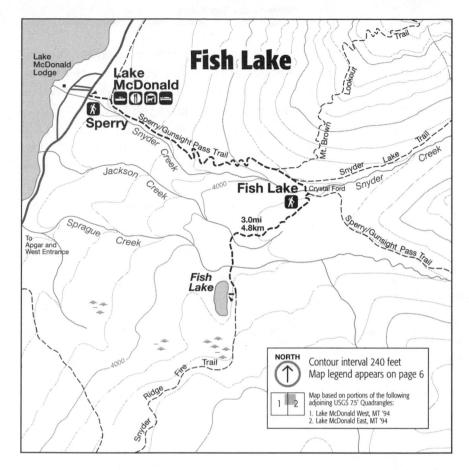

landform north of the lake. The trail then winds back into a forest of cedar, hemlock, Douglas fir, and western white pine.

Expect to encounter many hikers and backpackers along the trail. At 1.7 miles the number of hikers using the trail will begin to dwindle as some have chosen to access Mount Brown Lookout via that trail. Stay on the Gunsight Pass Trail. Within 0.1 mile the trail splits again. The trail to the left leads to Snyder Lake. Again, continue on the Gunsight Pass Trail. After 0.25 mile the trail crosses Snyder Creek at what is known as Crystal Ford on a well-constructed footbridge. There is another trail junction on the other side of the bridge. A sign identifies Sperry Trail and Snyder Ridge Fire Trail. Follow the Snyder Ridge Fire Trail to Fish Lake.

The Snyder Ridge Fire Trail is not shared with horses or the hikers accessing Sperry Glacier and Chalet and is narrower and has soft padding. This is a fairyland environment that will delight children. Surrounding you is a healthy mixed forest with a lot of ferns, wildflowers, and fungi growing on the forest floor. The trail follows Snyder Ridge and ascends and descends two drainages before reaching Fish Lake. The first drainage is Jackson Creek, which you'll cross on a footbridge. Notice, just before crossing the creek, the mature western hemlock tree with its roots wrapping around a large rock. The second drainage is Sprague Creek. You are now within a soccer field's distance of Fish Lake.

Fish Lake is in a deep forest setting. Trees grow at shoreline, affording you few opportunities to access the lake. From the point where the trail meets the lake you will see the blossoms of water lilies. Listen for frogs calling, and watch for common loons spending their days feeding at Fish Lake. Betraying its name, Fish Lake affords only fair fishing opportunities. This is an excellent destination for hikers seeking to stretch their legs or looking for a good place to have a picnic.

Twin Falls.

Rising Wolf Mountain.

Two Medicine Valley.

Two Medicine Lake.

Aster Falls.

Upper Two Medicine Lake.

Appistoki Falls.

Running Eagle Falls.

Medicine Grizzly Lake.

Cut Bank Valley.

Atlantic Falls.

Lake Josephine.

Cracker Lake.

Grinnell Peak.

Grinnell Lake.

Swiftcurrent Valley.

Grinnell Glacier.

Redrock Lake.

Appekunny Falls.

Appekunny Mountain.

Swiftcurrent Lake/Grinnell Valley.

Waterton Lake.

Haystack Butte.

Hidden Lake.

Going-to-the-Sun Mountain.

Avalanche Lake.

St. Mary Falls.

Red Eagle Lake.

Bowman Lake.

Logging Lake.

Quartz Lake.

Snyder Lake

Set in one of the most beautiful cirques west of the Continental Divide, the Snyder Lake area provides wonderful wildlife viewing opportunities.

Level of difficulty: Moderate.

Distance: 8.8 miles round trip.

Duration: 5–6 hours.

Best time of year: July–September.

Trailhead: Across from Lake McDonald Lodge on the south side of the Going-to-the-Sun Road. The trailhead is marked as "Sperry Trail."

Hiking directions: Enter the forest on Sperry Trail. You soon arrive at a sign that announces the trail as the Gunsight Pass Trail. Continue on this trail for 1.8 miles then turn left onto the Snyder Lake Trail.

Special attention: Sperry Trail is heavily traveled. Horseback riders and hikers accessing Fish Lake, Mount Brown Lookout, and the Sperry Chalet use the trail.

Notes: Sperry Trail was the first officially constructed trail in Glacier National Park. University of Minnesota Professor Lyman Sperry and a group of his students constructed the trail from what is now Lake McDonald Lodge to Sperry Glacier in 1902. They conducted the project *gratis,* for the pleasure of spending the summer in the mountains.

The forest near Going-to-the-Sun Road is made up of hemlock, western red cedar, and western larch. It has a high canopy, very few lower limbs. Because of the high canopy little direct sunlight penetrates the tree cover. Consequently, there is little understory. Nonetheless, the forest floor has masses of ferns, mosses, and fungi.

The trail is wide and offers soft footing. After 0.33 mile you come to an overlook of Snyder Creek. From here you can see the eastern part of the creek set beneath Howe Ridge and Lake McDonald. Lake McDonald is the largest lake in the park, 9.5 miles long and 1.5 miles at its greatest width. Its 400-foot depth makes it the deepest lake in Glacier. Lake McDonald was formed when rem-

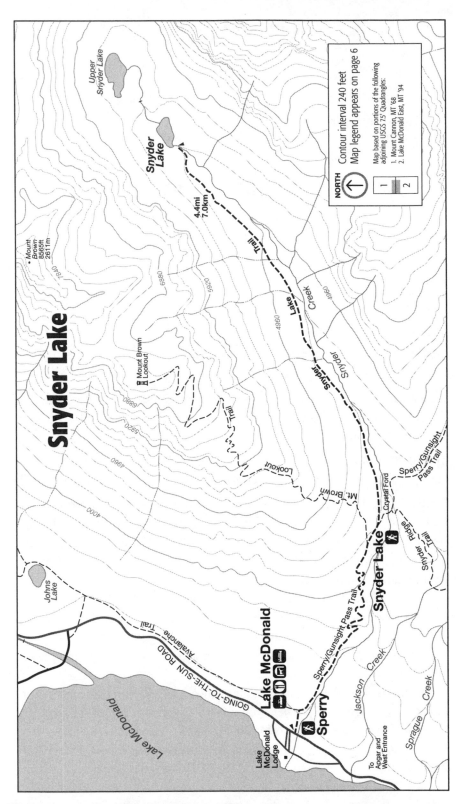

Snyder Lake

Upper Snyder Lake

Snyder Lake

4.4mi
7.0km

Mount Brown 8565ft 2611m

Mount Brown Lookout

Mt. Brown Lookout Trail

Snyder Lake Creek

Snyder Creek

Crystal Ford

Sperry/Gunsight Pass Trail

Snyder Lake

Snyder Ridge Trail

Johns Lake

Lake McDonald

Avalanche Trail

GOING-TO-THE-SUN ROAD

Lake McDonald

Sperry/Gunsight Pass Trail

Sperry

Jackson Creek

Sprague Creek

Lake McDonald Lodge

To Apgar and West Entrance

NORTH

Contour interval 240 feet
Map legend appears on page 6

Map based on portions of the following adjoining USGS 7.5' Quadrangles:

1. Mount Cannon, MT '68
2. Lake McDonald East, MT '94

1
2

nant ice from a mountain glacier settled at this spot and prevented sediments from the mountains from filling the depression. The historical Kootenai name for Lake McDonald is Sacred Dancing Lake—so named because every summer the tribes gathered there for their annual religious ceremonies.

The trail continues to wind up the ridge east of Snyder Creek. The trail will approach the ridge side two more times before heading up the canyon to Snyder Lake. The trail soon begins a series of switchbacks and winds into a closed forest with dense understory that includes snowberry and packed groundcover with many fungi. In this part of the forest western larch become more numerous.

At 2 miles you come to the Mount Brown Lookout Trail. It is a difficult 3.7-mile hike to the lookout.

About 100 feet beyond the Mount Brown Lookout Trail junction you encounter the Snyder Lake Trail and leave the Gunsight Pass Trail. You are approximately 2.5 miles from Snyder Lake.

The Snyder Lake Trail begins more narrowly than the Gunsight Pass Trail, with easy footing. Soon, the trail becomes increasingly rocky. From the trail junction to the lake the trail slowly climbs and runs diagonally across the southern base of Mount Brown. Snyder Creek is on your right. You will hear the water all the way to Snyder Lake.

The forest along this part of the trail is composed of hemlock, western larch, and spruce trees. The broadleaf tree species comprise the beautifully colorful mountain maple in autumn and the nitrogen fixer mountain alder.

Mountain alders are pioneer tree species that indicate recent disturbance to the soil, most likely from avalanches. The roots of alders contain bacteria that combine nitrogen with oxygen from the air and make it available in the soil. Alders are fast-growing and short-lived. They place nitrogen in the soil for other trees and allow forest succession to continue.

The forest understory includes Oregon grape, pearlyeverlasting, fireweed, cow parsnips, beargrass, huckleberry plants, asters, and bracken ferns.

As you approach the lake, the trail will become gradually damper with intermittent creeks. The forest floor is progressively more diverse with profuse annual plant growth. At times the understory of cow parsnips nearly overgrows the trail. Be cautious. Bears like cow parsnips. Make noise. The dense growth may conceal a bear.

Within 1 mile of the lake you will come to a large slope composed of thumb sized to fist-sized rock fragments. Known as a scree field it is home to pikas. A high-pitched short raspy bugle will alert you to the fact that you have been spotted. Notice the different patterns of growth and the color of the lichens

Snyder Lake and Little Matterhorn.

growing on the limestone rock of the scree. The normally gray rocks take on a green tinge due to the density of the lichens.

After passing the scree you break out into an area where you can see the lofty, shattered, limestone faces of 8,565-foot Mount Brown, 7,886-foot Little Matterhorn, and Mount Edwards. These three mountains form the cirque basin on three sides. You will find Snyder Lake in this cirque. The lake is named after George Snyder, who built a framed hotel at the present site of the Lake McDonald Lodge in 1885. The forest around the lake is mostly subalpine fir and alder.

You will hear water cascading from Little Matterhorn. There is a second Snyder Lake above the one you are visiting. It is about the same size as the lower lake. No established trails reach the upper lake.

Listen for pikas bugling near the head of the lake. Watch for mountain goats on the cliff faces of Mount Edwards. Look for signs of bears as you make your way back to the trailhead.

Pika

As you pass talus slopes you may hear a series of short bugle-like squeaks. The peculiar squeaks tell you that you are in the territory of the pika, one of the more elusive mammals of Glacier National Park Often referred to as rock rabbits, these grapefruit-sized mammals live among the rocks. Pikas are colonial members of the rabbit family and feed on grasses and the stems of wildflowers. It is fun to search talus slopes for small piles of their food laid on rocks to dry in the sun. When the food is dry they store it underground. Pikas are active year round, living in the talus slopes and scree fields under the winter snow and eating the food they harvested and stored. People find them particularly charming because pikas look like a ball of fur without a tail and have very small ears and a rabbit's face. Listen and look for them throughout Glacier's high country.

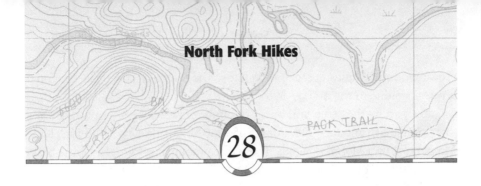
Forest and Fire Nature Trail

Previously known as the Huckleberry Mountain Nature Trail, this trail's new name reflects the National Park Service's commitment to the story of fire in natural environments.

Level of difficulty: Easy.

Distance: 0.9 mile round trip.

Duration: 1 hour.

Best time of year: June–October.

Trailhead: Turn south on the paved road between the Camas Creek entrance station and the Glacier National Park entrance sign. Follow the road to a large parking area.

Hiking directions: Follow the Forest and Fire Nature Trail signs. The trail begins at the southern end of the parking lot.

Notes: The Glacier Natural History Association and the National Park Service have provided a trail guide. You can acquire the guide for 50 cents at the trailhead.

For many years the Huckleberry Mountain Nature Trail was a favorite walk for many visitors to Glacier National Park. It led through a forest regenerating from a fire in the late 1960s. Visitors experienced a young and vibrant forest environment of lodgepole pine, western larch, fireweed, and grasses. People also came to Huckleberry Mountain to catch sight of the myriad animals that found food and cover in the forest—animals such as deer, elk, bear, and mice.

The forest succession process abruptly started over again between August and October of 2001. Another forest fire swept through the area. Known as the Moose Fire it burned hotter than the previous conflagration. In some places, the fire consumed all of the vegetation. Trees that survived the fire in the 1960s were killed in the Moose Fire.

The forest that burned in the 1960s was composed mostly of lodgepole pine and western larch. A mature western larch has bark 3–6 inches thick and has little resin. Consequently, it is resistant to fire damage. However, most of the western larches were killed in the Moose Fire, and another tree, the lodgepole pine,

102

Forest and Fire Nature Trail

To
Going-to-the-Sun
Road

Camas Creek
Entrance

3400

**Forest and Fire
Nature Trail**

CAMAS ROAD

3600

0.9mi
1.4km
Loop

NORTH

Contour interval 40 feet
Map legend appears on page 6

To
Outside North
Fork Road

| 1 | 2 |
| 3 | 4 |

Map based on portions of the following
adjoining USGS 7.5' Quadrangles:

1. Demers Ridge, MT '94
2. Camas Ridge West, MT '68
3. Huckleberry Mountain, MT '94
4. McGee Meadow, MT '94

will be the pioneer conifer in this immediate area of the forest. Like the western larch, the lodgepole pine has its own unique adaptation to fire. The individual trees are not fire resistant and easily die in the flames. Nonetheless, they have specialized cones that are sealed and protected in pitch until the pitch is melted in a fire. The cones open after a fire and release the seed to the wind. Lodgepole pine seeds are among the first to germinate on a new forest bed. Other trees to establish themselves quickly after a fire are the black cottonwood and the aspen. The pioneer flowering plants include Bicknell's geranium, Canada thistle, spirea, pinegrass, wild strawberries, corydalis, and asters. Look for small shoots of these plants.

As you might have guessed, this forest burns on a recurring basis. It may be many years before another significant fire event alters the landscape. Until then, return repeatedly to the Forest and Fire Nature Trail and observe how the forest environment proceeds through the succession process.

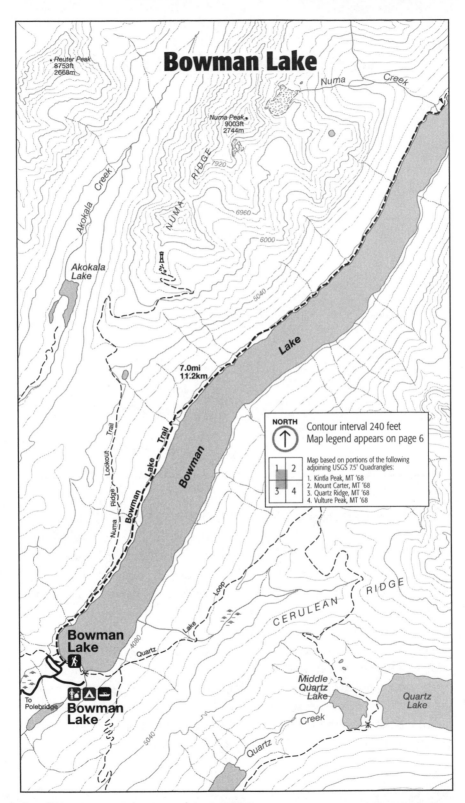

Bowman Lake

Reuter Peak
8753ft
2668m

Numa Creek

Numa Peak
9003ft
2744m

N U M A   R I D G E

7920

6960

6000

Akokala Creek

Akokala
Lake

5040

Lake

7.0mi
11.2km

Bowman

Bowman Lake Trail

Lookout Trail

Numa Ridge Trail

NORTH

Contour interval 240 feet
Map legend appears on page 6

1	2
3	4

Map based on portions of the following
adjoining USGS 7.5' Quadrangles:

1. Kintla Peak, MT '68
2. Mount Carter, MT '68
3. Quartz Ridge, MT '68
4. Vulture Peak, MT '68

Loop

Lake

C E R U L E A N   R I D G E

4080

**Bowman
Lake**

Quartz

To
Polebridge

**Bowman
Lake**

5040

Middle
Quartz
Lake

Quartz
Lake

Creek

Quartz

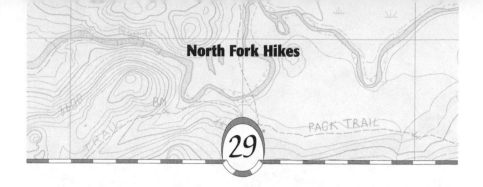

Bowman Lake

Skirting the northern shore of Bowman Lake, this trail provides a superb stroll along a magnificent lakeshore.

Level of difficulty: Moderate.

Distance: 14 miles round trip.

Duration: 2–7 hours.

Best time of year: June–October.

Trailhead: The Bowman Lake Trailhead is north of the boat launch at Bowman Lake.

Hiking directions: The trail is well marked along the north shore of Bowman Lake.

Special attention: This is a frequently used trail so expect to encounter other visitors enjoying the walk.

Notes: Although the trail is 7 miles to the end of the lake you may wish to walk only part way. This is a popular stroll for visitors staying in the Bowman Lake Campground or people who have come to Bowman Lake for a picnic. It provides a great early morning or evening walk. There are several access points to the lake where you can soak your feet or let your children play. The trail is infrequently exposed to direct sunlight, making this a desirable trail to follow even on a bright, hot, summer day.

Glacier is known for its beautiful red and green argillite rocks. North of the boat launch, you will find a beach with a magnificent collection of quarter-sized, flat, red and green rocks smoothed by the wave action of the lake.

After leaving the beach, you will pass a large log building on your left. This is the Bowman Lake ranger station, but it wasn't always used for this purpose. The chalet-like building was known as Rainbow Lodge, and it is the only remaining structure of Skyland Camp. In the early 1920s Colonel L.R. Gignilliat, the superintendent of Culver Military Academy in Indiana, secured a five-year contract with the National Park Service to build a summer camp for the cadets

Bowman Lake.

of his academy. The camp, known as Skyland, had several structures, most of which were located at the site of the present Bowman Lake Campground. Concerns over mismanagement convinced the Superintendent of Glacier National Park to not renew the contract. The site languished from 1929 to 1940, when the National Park Service razed all of the buildings except for the chalet. This beautiful building became the ranger station.

Beyond this piece of history the trail passes through a forest of lodgepole pine, spruce, subalpine fir, western larch, and mountain maple. The forest floor is rich with low-growing shrubs, wildflowers, mosses, and ferns. This area is home to red squirrels, chipmunks, deer, bears, and several species of birds. Watch for waterfowl along the shoreline of the lake.

The trail is wide with good, soft footing. You can enjoy wonderful views of the southest mountains rimming the lake, including 9,843-foot Thunderbird Mountain, Mount Carter, and 9,891-foot Rainbow Peak. The low ridge to the south is Cerulean Ridge. Study the ridge and speculate why ancestral Kootenai named it Bear Hat Mountain.

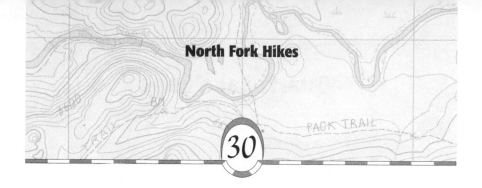

Quartz Lake Loop

This is one of the few loop trails in Glacier National Park. It takes you through deep forest, forest burned in the 1988 Red Bench Fire, and to three lovely lakes nestled between Cerulean Ridge to the north and Logging Ridge to the south.

Level of difficulty: Strenuous.

Distance: 12.8 miles round trip.

Duration: 7–8 hours.

Best time of year: June–September.

Trailhead: The trail begins at the south end of the boat launch area at Bowman Lake.

Hiking directions: Since this is a loop trail you may choose to hike either clockwise or counter-clockwise. It is advised that you take the clockwise option. After 0.4 mile take the lefthand trail to begin the loop.

Notes: The first 0.2 mile of the trail follows the southwest shore of Bowman Lake then crosses Bowman Creek on a well-constructed footbridge. In the early morning or late evening, you may hear songbirds in this area.

The trail follows the southern shore of Bowman Lake and gradually begins an ascent to the crest of Cerulean Ridge 2.5 miles from the trailhead. This part of the trail is on the northern side of the ridge through a cool and damp spruce-fir forest interspersed with western larch trees.

The north-facing Cerulean Ridge has a low-growing understory of bearberry, thimbleberry, twinflower, bunchberry, dogwood, snowberry, myriad moss species, liverworts, and mushrooms.

After another 0.4 mile you come to the trail junction that begins the loop. Go to the left toward Quartz Lake Campground. The sign lists the campground at 5.8 miles.

After another 2.5 miles the trail reaches the crest of Cerulean Ridge and levels out, following the ridgeline. The trail soon drops into the Quartz Creek drainage and enters part of the forest effected by the 38,000-acre Red Bench

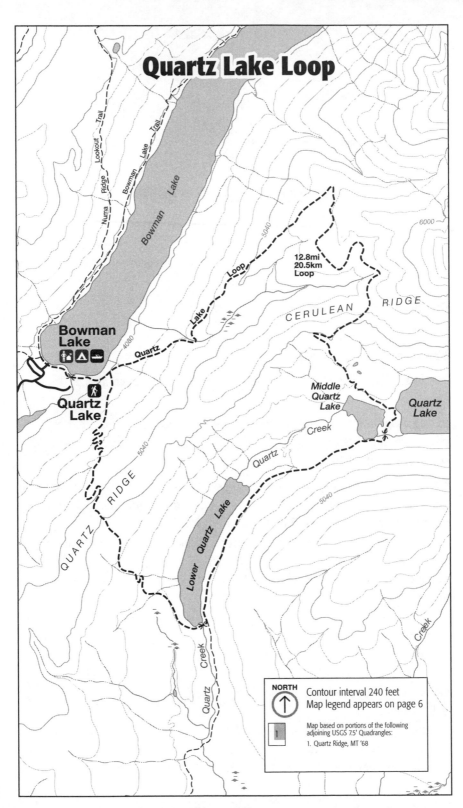

Quartz Lake Loop

Lookout Trail

Numa Ridge

Bowman Lake Trail

Bowman Lake

Loop

Lake

5040

12.8mi
20.5km
Loop

6000

CERULEAN RIDGE

Bowman Lake

Quartz

4080

Quartz Lake

Middle Quartz Lake

Creek

Quartz

Lake

QUARTZ RIDGE

5040

Quartz

Lower Quartz Lake

5040

Quartz Creek

Creek

NORTH

Contour interval 240 feet
Map legend appears on page 6

Map based on portions of the following
adjoining USGS 7.5' Quadrangles:

1. Quartz Ridge, MT '68

Fire of September 1988. This part of the trail is your first opportunity to see vistas of mountains extending into the distance until the peaks dissolve at the edge of an intense blue sky. The ridge to the immediate south with an equal elevation to where you are walking is Logging Ridge. The mountains to the west make up the Whitefish Range in the Flathead National Forest. Below you, you can see Lower Quartz Lake, Middle Quartz Lake, and the western part of Quartz Lake.

On a sunny day the microclimate of the southern exposure of Cerulean Ridge will be noticeably different from the forest you have been walking in for the last hour. This ridge-side illustrates the rejuvenation of the forest. Pioneer plants such as fireweed and lodgepole pine have taken hold. If you return to this area periodically in the next few years, you will witness the trees growing from shoulder height to several stories tall. You will observe that more long-lived understory perennial plants, such as beargrass, have replaced the fireweed.

As you descend the ridge it will appear that you are about to run into Middle Quartz Lake. Instead, you will turn to the east before reaching Middle Quartz and arrive at Quartz Lake Campground. The campground is situated on the western shore of this large lake. The shoreline here is beachlike. It is a good place to stop, rest, eat a snack, and enjoy the mountains looming over the eastern shore. The prominent peaks from left to right are 9,891-foot Rainbow Peak, 8,128-foot Redhorn Peak, 9,638-foot Vulture Peak, and 8,566-foot Logging Mountain.

After leaving the campground you will encounter a sign that announces Quartz Creek Trail. Follow Quartz Creek Trail to the right. The trail skirts the southern shore of Middle Quartz Lake. After about 1 mile you arrive at the head of Lower Quartz Lake. The trail works its way around the eastern side, never quite reaching the shoreline. At about 9.5 miles you will cross Quartz Creek on a footbridge. The trail leaves the water and begins the long climb over Quartz Ridge. Most of the trail to the top of the ridge is through forest burned in the Red Bench Fire. At the top of the ridge you will be rewarded with extensive views of the Livingston Range to the east and the Apgar Mountains and the Whitefish Range to the west. On a clear day you will be able to identify the distinctive pinnacle of Great Northern Peak in the Great Bear Wilderness far to the south in the Flathead National Forest.

The remainder of the loop is downhill. You have crossed over Quartz Ridge and will be hiking through the lovely, deep, cool forest of the Bowman Valley drainage.

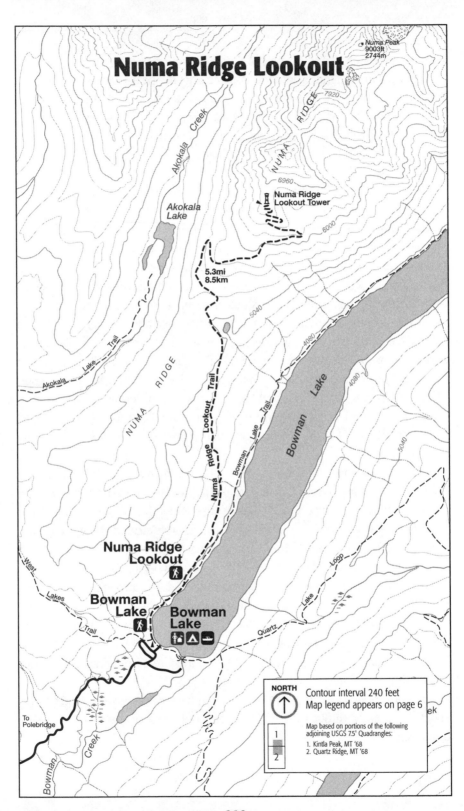

Numa Ridge Lookout

Numa Peak
9003ft
2744m

7920

N U M A   R I D G E

6960

Numa Ridge
Lookout Tower

Akokala Creek

Akokala
Lake

6000

5.3mi
8.5km

5040

4080

Bowman Lake

4080

Akokala Lake Trail

Akokala

N U M A   R I D G E

Numa Ridge Lookout Trail

Bowman Lake Trail

5040

Loop

Lake

Numa Ridge
Lookout

Bowman
Lake

West

Lakes

Bowman
Lake

Trail

Quartz

To
Polebridge

Bowman Creek

NORTH Contour interval 240 feet
Map legend appears on page 6

Map based on portions of the following
adjoining USGS 7.5' Quadrangles:

1. Kintla Peak, MT '68
2. Quartz Ridge, MT '68

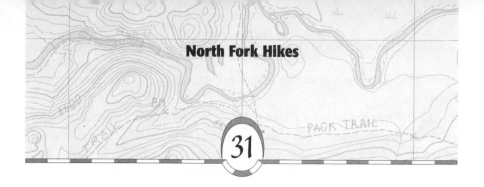

Numa Ridge Lookout

Anticipate splendid views from a fire lookout. Numa Ridge Lookout is a steep but worthwhile hike.

Level of difficulty: Strenuous.

Distance: 10.6 miles round trip.

Duration: 6–7 hours.

Best time of year: July–October.

Trailhead: The trail begins north of the Bowman Lake boat launch. The trail is marked as the Bowman Lake Trail.

Hiking directions: Follow the Bowman Lake Trail for 0.7 mile then turn left onto the Numa Ridge Lookout Trail.

Special attention: Take plenty of water. There is no water available at the lookout. You will be walking on partially exposed south-facing slopes. Dehydration can occur quickly. Start your hike early in the day.

Notes: Your hike begins on the pleasant Bowman Lake Trail. This trail follows the north shore of Bowman Lake through a mixed and mature forest of lodgepole pine, spruce, Douglas fir, western larch, and mountain maple. The forest floor has a wealth of low-growing shrubs, wildflowers, ferns, mosses, and fungus. Notice the numerous tree trunks lying on the forest floor in various stages of decay. Sooner or later all of these trunks will become soil as the fungus, ferns, mosses, and larger plants break down the wood.

The Numa Ridge Lookout Trail climbs directly into the forest. You will not see Bowman Lake again for several miles. The forest is little changed from that of the Bowman Lake Trail. This part of the forest is home to red squirrels, woodpeckers, gray jays, sapsuckers, robins, chickadees, and nuthatches. Look for 1- to 2-inch-long dark droppings on the trail. These droppings are from ruffed grouse.

Approximately 2.7 miles from the trailhead you pass Moose Pond. You can see this small body of water to your right and through the trees. The pond is lined with aquatic plants including water lilies. There is no established access to the pond. Moose Pond is a prevailing feature in the landscape as you look west from the lookout.

The trail remains level for a brief distance, angles to the east, and then begins to climb. Soon you are walking on several long switchbacks. The steepest part of the climb is the partially exposed south-facing slope of Numa Ridge.

The trail bed turns from the soft footing of the forest to broken limestone

Numa Ridge Lookout Tower.

near the lookout. This is prime habitat for pikas, Clark's nutcrackers, and falcons. After reaching the 6,960-foot Numa Ridge Lookout you can see the distinctive shape of Moose Pond sitting on Numa Ridge. To the north and below you in the Akokala Creek drainage is Akokala Lake. You will also have splendid views of the Whitefish Range to the west and the Livingston Range to the east. To the east and the southeast is 9,843-foot Mount Carter and 9,891-foot Rainbow Peak. To the north is Reuter Peak at 8,763 feet and looming in front of you is Numa Peak at 9,003 feet.

At the lookout you are close enough to Reuter Peak and Numa Peak that you will not need binoculars to spot the deer, elk, and bears that frequent the mountain faces near timberline. However, a pair of binoculars can make your search more exciting.

Finally, you may be happy to learn that it will take about half the time to reach the trailhead as it did to hike to the summit.

Grouse

You are walking through a forest with dense undergrowth. Without forewarning you hear a thunderous explosion of wings beating the air only a few feet in front of you. Startled, you stop to allow your pulse to go back to normal rate. You have just experienced a ruffed grouse escaping your menacing presence.

The grouse knew you were coming. But the chicken-sized bird is so "tame" that it did not get out of the way of potential danger until the last moment. As you watch what some people call a fool-hen escape, you can see it flies about as well as a chicken. And if it lands in the boughs of a spruce tree you will notice it is not particularly adapted to standing in trees.

So what do grouse do in addition to startle hikers? They eat small insects and seeds, but probably their most interesting behavior is the way the male attracts a female. He performs a wing-beating ritual while standing on a log. He begins slowly beating his wings front to back as if he intends to fly. Within 15 seconds he produces a fast drumming sound. The log he has chosen to stand on is known as a "drumming log." If the log is hollow the sound is more resonant. He may have as many as three drumming logs in his territory.

Listen for the deep sounds of the male grouse drumming as you walk through the forest in the springtime and early summer. The sound may at first seem ethereal and difficult to pinpoint. With attentiveness you might be able to locate where the drumming is coming from and spy on the male carrying out this enthralling ritual.

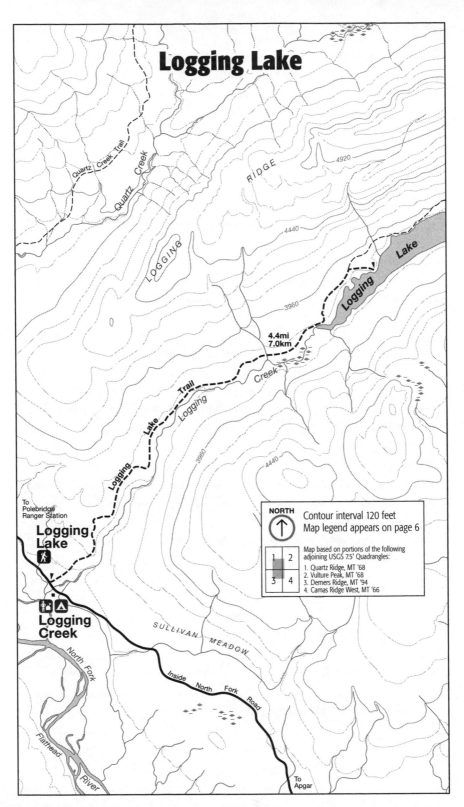

Logging Lake

RIDGE

4920

Quartz Creek Trail

Quartz Creek

4440

LOGGING

Lake

Logging

3960

**4.4mi
7.0km**

Creek

Logging

Lake

Trail

Logging

3960

4440

To
Polebridge
Ranger Station

**Logging
Lake**

**Logging
Creek**

SULLIVAN MEADOW

North Fork

Inside North Fork Road

Flathead

River

To
Apgar

NORTH Contour interval 120 feet
Map legend appears on page 6

Map based on portions of the following
adjoining USGS 7.5' Quadrangles:

1	2
3	4

1. Quartz Ridge, MT '68
2. Vulture Peak, MT '68
3. Demers Ridge, MT '94
4. Camas Ridge West, MT '66

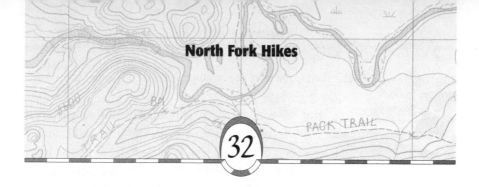

32

Logging Lake

Far from the scores of tourists traveling Going-to-the-Sun Road, Logging Lake receives relatively few visitors. The trail takes you through an undisturbed forest to a regenerating forest, and finally to a typical North Fork lake set amid towering peaks.

Level of difficulty: Moderate.

Distance: 8.8 miles round trip.

Duration: 4–5 hours.

Best time of year: June–October.

Trailhead: The trailhead is next to Logging Creek Campground and the Logging Creek ranger station, approximately 7 miles south of the Polebridge entrance station on Inside North Fork Road. There is parking space for six vehicles.

Hiking directions: Follow Logging Creek Trail directly to Logging Lake.

Special attention: The trail traverses through a forest burned by the 1988 Red Bench Fire. Carry plenty of drinking water with you, especially during summer.

Notes: The trail follows the north side of Logging Creek and is a narrow winding path with soft, easy footing. Listen for the rattle of kingfishers along Logging Creek. This montane forest is mixed with spruce, western larch, Douglas fir, ponderosa pine, and redoiser dogwood. The forest understory includes lush grasses intermingled with wild strawberry, fireweed, thimbleberry, snowberry, kinnikinnick, lupine, wild rose, queencup, asters, bearberry, juniper, pearlyeverlasting, and Oregon grape.

After 0.25 mile you will enter an area of the forest altered by the 1988 Red Bench Fire. The fire in this immediate part of the forest did not kill the larger ponderosa pines and western larch trees. They were spared because the fire was not hot enough to reach the crown of the trees. However, most of the smaller trees were killed because their lower branches were close to the forest floor. This allowed the fire to climb up the trees in a ladder effect and consume all of the branches. Farther up the trail you will pass through a part of the forest in which the flames reached the crown and all of the larger trees were killed.

This burned-over part of the forest is today illustrative of the regeneration process that occurs after a fire. Small lodgepole pines and fir trees are beginning to take hold. The undergrowth is flourishing with fireweed and alder trees.

After 1.5 miles you reenter the unaffected forest. The margin between the two areas provides a good contrast between an undisturbed forest and one changed by fire. The remainder of your walk will be through a mature mixed spruce-fir forest with healthy undergrowth.

At 4.2 miles you will come to a sign directing you to the Logging Lake Campground. The sign shows the way to a lovely cove on the northern shore of the lake. At one time Logging Lake carried the name Big Beaver Lake. Indian legend describes a 20-foot-long beaver found in the lake. The mountains in view at the eastern end of the lake are from left to right: 8,566-foot Logging Mountain, 8,375-foot Mount Geduhn, 8,279-foot Anaconda Mountain, and 7,802-foot Wolf Gun Mountain. The low ridgeline to the south is Adair Ridge.

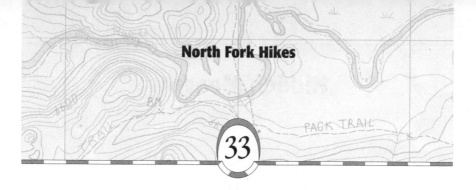

Hidden Meadow

The Hidden Meadow Trail provides a short stroll to an out-of-the-way meadow with abundant wildlife.

Level of difficulty: Easy.

Distance: 2.4 miles round trip.

Duration: 1–2 hours.

Best time of year: June–September.

Trailhead: The trailhead is across from Lone Pine Prairie, on Inside North Fork Road. There is parking for five vehicles at the trailhead.

Hiking directions: Follow the Hidden Meadow Trail to Hidden Meadow.

Special attention: This is moose and black bear country. Do not approach these animals.

Notes: The trail passes through the effects of the Red Bench Fire of 1988 for the first mile. Lodgepole pines have established themselves as the dominant tree species. Note the size of the trees and how tall they have grown since 1988. Also notice the remaining snags of the trees that were killed by the fire. How many years will it take for the new forest to be as tall as the former forest? You may find pieces of farming equipment off the trail. This area was homesteaded before it was part of Glacier National Park. The trail terminates at a large out-of-the-way meadow surrounding a series of shallow lakes. A lone, massive, old-growth Douglas fir marks the end of the trail. The vicinity near the meadow is dominated by a young aspen grove. Look for evidence of bears, elk, and deer. Listen for the sounds of male ruffed grouse drumming if you are visiting this area in the springtime or early summer.

In the meadow you can find wildflowers such as penstemons, arrow-leaved balsam root, northern mule-ears, larkspurs, and fleabanes.

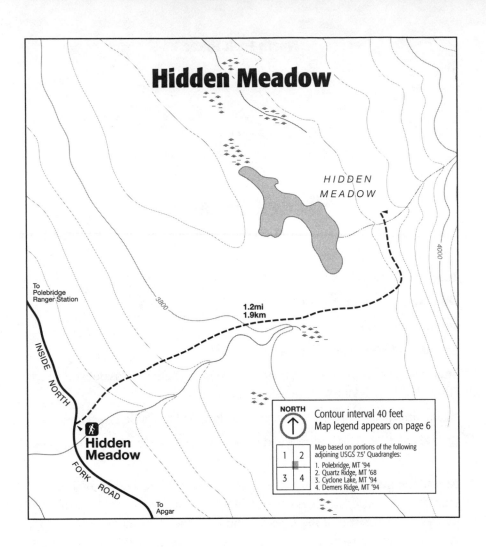

Hidden Meadow

*HIDDEN
MEADOW*

4000

To
Polebridge
Ranger Station

3800

1.2mi
1.9km

INSIDE NORTH

Hidden
Meadow

FORK ROAD

To
Apgar

NORTH

Contour interval 40 feet
Map legend appears on page 6

Map based on portions of the following
adjoining USGS 7.5' Quadrangles:

1	2
3	4

1. Polebridge, MT '94
2. Quartz Ridge, MT '68
3. Cyclone Lake, MT '94
4. Demers Ridge, MT '94

Lodgepole Pine

Pinus contorta. Those familiar with Latin will recognize this as "contorted pine"—an unlikely scientific name for a tree that grows so straight that Native Americans have historically used it for lodge building. Lodgepole pine trunks probably hold up the tepees you see erected outside the park. Although great portions of Glacier National Park are comprised of lodgepole pine forests the scientists who first described these trees were studying the lodgepole pines living on the Pacific North Coast. These trees, genetically similar to the lodgepole pines in Glacier, grow in a contorted way. Their twisted growth pattern is due to the local environment of cool maritime winds and salt air. In Glacier, stands of young lodgepole pine trees can grow so straight and close together that they are referred to as "dog-hair."

Lodgepole pines are slow-growing, have thin bark, and have slowly developing seeds. They rarely live more than 200 years. The trees are easily killed by fire. Lodgepole pine forests are fire dependent; they need to burn periodically in order to be rejuvenated. An advantage lodgepole pines have over other trees is that the heat from fires opens their pinecones and allows the seeds to fall on the freshly burned forest floor. Often lodgepole pines are the first coniferous trees to become established after a forest fire.

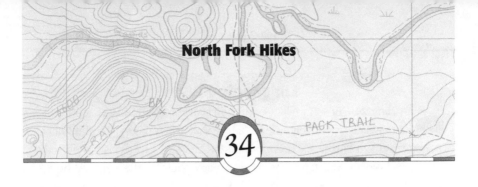

Covey Meadow Loop

Covey Meadow is one of several meadows along the North Fork. The loop trail provides easy access to a great vista and an interesting wildlife habitat.

Level of difficulty: Easy.

Distance: 2 miles round trip.

Duration: 1–2 hours.

Best time of year: July–October.

Trailhead: The Covey Meadow Loop Trailhead is located 0.5 mile south of the Polebridge entrance station on Inside North Fork Road. You will find the trailhead on the east side of the road. There is parking for one vehicle on the west side of road.

Hiking directions: The trail is very distinct at the trailhead and easy to follow to its termination. After leaving Covey Meadow the trail reenters the forest regenerating from the Red Bench Fire and makes its way back to Inside North Fork Road. The trail reaches the road near the Polebridge ranger station. You will have to walk south along the road for nearly 0.5 mile to arrive at your starting point.

Special attention: This is bear country. This trail is frequently closed in the early part of visitor season due to bear sightings.

Notes: The trail traverses a forest altered by the Red Bench Fire of September 7, 1988. Notice the nearly uniform height of the lodgepole pines that have become established. Lodgepole pines grow close together in a pattern known as "dog-hair." The few tall trees that tower over the dog-hair are western larch. They were mature when the fire swept through this area. Because of their thick bark and lack of lower branches they were able to resist the flames. Also observe that the undergrowth is made up mostly of grasses. This is because the forest is not mature enough to support a diverse understory.

The trail cuts through the lodgepole forest until it reaches an old river bench. This area can be very wet in June and early July. The trail follows the bottom of

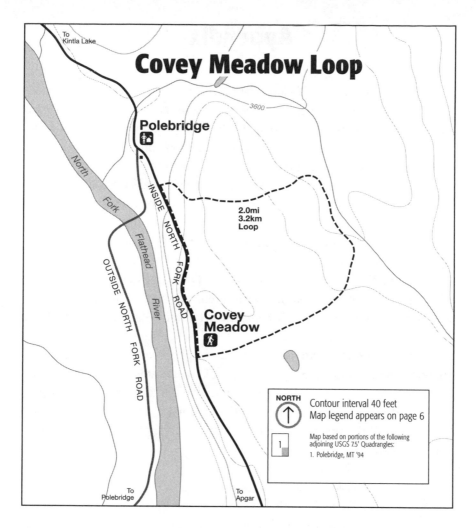

Covey Meadow Loop

To
Kintla Lake

Polebridge

North Fork

INSIDE NORTH FORK ROAD

Flathead River

OUTSIDE NORTH FORK ROAD

3600

2.0mi
3.2km
Loop

Covey
Meadow

NORTH
↑

Contour interval 40 feet
Map legend appears on page 6

Map based on portions of the following
adjoining USGS 7.5' Quadrangles:
1. Polebridge, MT '94

To
Polebridge

To
Apgar

the ancient creek to Covey Meadow. The meadow provides a spectacular display of wildflowers and meadow grasses, and an unhindered view of the Livingston Range to the east. Inconspicuously positioning yourself on the margin of the meadow in the early morning hours will permit you to view the myriad wildlife that visit this meadow. You will perhaps see elk, deer, bears, foxes, coyotes, Columbian ground squirrels, and many bird species.

Appendix

The spectacular Glacier National Park environment has captured the attention and imagination of people for hundreds of years. Native Americans have long had attachments to this land, and it has helped fashion their world-view. The Anglo-European perspective has evolved from one of indifference, to curiosity, to exploitation, and more recently to stewardship.

Numerous citizens championed the cause of setting aside the Glacier area for the enjoyment of future generations. Since the park was established in 1910, people working for the National Park Service, park concessionaire employees, the park's neighboring residents, the Blackfeet Nation, and private nonprofit associations have carried forward the vision of Glacier's importance to human enrichment.

Today, there are several organizations actively working to enhance the vision of Glacier National Park. You may wish to contact these organizations if your visits to the park inspire you to become involved with their preservation efforts.

The National Park Service has protected and preserved Glacier's natural and cultural resources since 1916, six years after Glacier became a national park. The National Park Service provides visitor information, interpretive naturalist programs, and visitor safety assistance. The Park Service also offers the popular Volunteers-in-Parks program and the Student Temporary Employment Program (STEP) in Glacier.

> The National Park Service
> Glacier National Park
> West Glacier, MT 59936
> www.nps.gov/glac/home.htm

Glacier National Park Associates is a private, nonprofit advocacy group that helps Glacier National Park accomplish its wide-ranging goals: promoting volunteer efforts, facilitating donations to accomplish projects, and educating the public about the natural and cultural resources of the park.

> Glacier National Park Associates
> P.O. Box 91
> Kalispell, MT 59903
> suejim@bigsky.net

The Glacier Natural History Association (GNHA) is a nonprofit cooperating association of the National Park Service. GNHA supports Glacier National Park's educational, interpretive, cultural, and scientific programs. The support it generates is acquired through sales at its bookstores in the visitor centers and ranger stations throughout the park, the bookstore at the GNHA Web site, its mail-order catalog, and by means of annual membership fees.

Glacier Natural History Association
Belton Depot/P.O. Box 310
West Glacier, MT 59936
gnha@glacierassociation.org
www.glacierassociation.org

The Glacier Institute is a private, nonprofit outdoor education organization intended to link visitors with the natural and cultural marvels of the Glacier ecosystem. Since 1983, the Institute has been providing field-related educational opportunities during the visitor season.

The Glacier Institute
137 Main Street/P.O. Box 7457
Kalispell, MT 59904
glacinst@digisys.net

The Student Conservation Association (SCA) is the nation's leading provider of conservation service opportunities and outdoor skills and leadership training for youth. Every year, high school and college students work on projects that might include visitor services, interpreting park natural and cultural history through talks and guided hikes, working at an information desk, and assisting with resource management programs.

The Student Conservation Association
689 River Road/P.O. Box 550
Charlestown, New Hampshire 03603-0550
www.thesca.org

The Glacier Fund is a nonprofit fund-raising partner for Glacier National Park. Funds benefit education projects, wildlife research, restoration of historic buildings, and backcountry trail projects. The Glacier Fund has established an endowment to help preserve the fleet of red tourist buses.

The Glacier Fund
P.O. Box 14
West Glacier, MT 59936

Glossary

Arête: A sharp-edged mountain ridge carved by a glacier.

Cirque: A natural amphitheater high on a mountain that was formed by the erosion at the head of a glacier.

Flagging: Trees killed above the snowline due to the dry effects of the wind and the lack of available water in the frozen soil. The branches below the snow pack are protected from the drying wind and remain alive.

Glacial flour: Tiny pieces of rock excavated by glaciers that are suspended in mountain lakes. Glacial flour gives a milky color to the water.

Horn: A mountain peak that has been carved by glaciers on more than one side resulting in a pointed summit.

Krumholz: At timberline, trees such as subalpine fir will grow in a low, gnarled, ground-hugging form. This form is known as Krumholz.

Park: A large meadow or grassland area surrounded by trees.

Riparian: Habitat situated along or near a river or stream.

Scree: Pieces of rock the size of an adult's thumb to the size of an adult's fist that have accumulated at the base of a mountain slope.

Sill: A more or less horizontal layer of igneous rock forced between layers of sedimentary rock or older volcanic beds.

Tarn: A small lake in the mountains.

Talus Slope: An accumulation of rock fragments, larger than scree, at the base of a mountain slope.

Index